ALASKA

By Bern Keating

Illustrations by National Geographic Photographer George F. Mobley

Produced by the National Geographic Special Publications Division,
Robert L. Breeden, Chief

National Geographic Society, Washington, D. C.
Melvin M. Payne, President
Melville Bell Grosvenor, Editor-in-Chief
Gilbert M. Grosvenor, Editor

ALASKA

By BERN KEATING
Photographs by GEORGE F. MOBLEY

Published by
THE NATIONAL GEOGRAPHIC SOCIETY
MELVIN M. PAYNE, *President*
MELVILLE BELL GROSVENOR, *Editor-in-Chief*
GILBERT M. GROSVENOR, *Editor*
WILLIAM GRAVES, *Consulting Editor*
    for this book

Prepared by
THE SPECIAL PUBLICATIONS DIVISION
ROBERT L. BREEDEN, *Editor*
DONALD J. CRUMP, *Associate Editor*
LEON M. LARSON, *Manuscript Editor*
JOHANNA G. FARREN, *Research*
LINDA M. BRIDGE, *Research Assistant*
PENELOPE W. SPRINGER, *Illustrations
    Research*
RICHARD M. CRUM, RONALD M. FISHER,
    LOUISE GRAVES, MAVIS KENNEDY,
    GERALD S. SNYDER, *Picture Legends*
MARY ANN HARRELL, *Style*
DOROTHY M. CORSON, JOLENE McCOY,
    Index
JUDITH C. FORD, CAROL R. TEACHEY,
    SANDRA A. TURNER, BARBARA J.
    WALKER, *Editorial Assistants*

Illustrations
BRYAN HODGSON, *Picture Editor*
JOHN J. BREHM, BETTY CLONINGER, JOHN
    D. GARST, JR., SNEJINKA STEFANOFF,
    Map Research and Production

Art Direction
JOSEPH A. TANEY, *Art Director*
JOSEPHINE B. BOLT, *Assistant Art Director*

Production and Printing
ROBERT W. MESSER, *Production Manager*
JUDY L. STRONG, *Production Assistant*
JAMES R. WHITNEY, *Engraving and Printing*
JOHN R. METCALFE, *Assistant, Engraving
    and Printing*

Standard Book Number 87044-076-4
Library of Congress Catalog Number 77-90215.

Second Edition 1971

*Wheeled camper rolls along an Alaska highway,
a slender thread that winds past gleaming peaks,
flower-strewn valleys, and the green of uncounted
spruce in the immense 49th State. Overleaf: Raven,
mythical hero of the Tlingit Indians, tops a totem
pole near Ketchikan; his wings shelter three children of the Sun. Page 1: Polaris and the Big
Dipper, stars ever present in Alaska's night skies
to guide voyagers, spangle the state flag, gold on
a field of blue. Endsheets: Shaped from luminous
particles, the aurora borealis spreads its puls-
ing veil over the Great Land. Book binding:
Staring eyes of a stylized bird dominate a Tlingit heraldic design, originally carved in leather.*

W. E. GARRETT, NATIONAL GEOGRAPHIC STAFF (RIGHT). DUST JACKET,
ENDSHEETS, AND OVERLEAF, NATIONAL GEOGRAPHIC PHOTOGRAPHER
GEORGE F. MOBLEY. PAGE 1, TOM DEFEO

Foreword

On a recent visit to Alaska I discovered that the 49th State is both an enchanting and a frustrating land. Enchanting in its immense beauty, size, and variety, and frustrating for much the same reasons—the average visitor, with only a few days or weeks to spend, sees only a tiny portion of its 586,400 square miles. Whatever the portion, it is likely to be memorable. Mine included a solitary evening beside a small lake in the southeastern, or panhandle, region and a five-pound rainbow trout that arched from the still water to take the fly.

There are other memories, but far too few of them; I want a great deal more of Alaska. So, too, do thousands of members of the Society, judging by their letters urging publication of a book on our largest state. In response, the Society has produced this richly illustrated volume that to me presents the enchantment without the frustration—its 208 colorful pages *are* Alaska.

To capture Alaska in all its breadth and detail, the Society commissioned a gifted free-lance author, Bern Keating, to roam the 49th State with George Mobley, one of the National Geographic's ablest staff photographers. Four months and 11,000 miles of travel produced some startling discoveries.

Mr. Keating found that Alaska today reflects many chapters from the Nation's past. Homesteading that stimulated settlement of the early West continues in the 49th State. Railroads and highways have barely penetrated the vast interior. An industrial revolution threatens to trap native populations—Indian, Aleut, and Eskimo—in a cultural squeeze between the proud past and an uncertain future. The historic lure of gold has given way to a rush for oil on Alaska's rich north slope. A series of wells in the Prudhoe Bay area west of Barter Island has responsible geologists estimating reserves of the field at ten billion barrels—nearly twice as large as the east-Texas field, previously the largest in North America.

During my visit I flew by floatplane north from Ketchikan in the panhandle into the vastness of Tongass National Forest. My companion was Pete Cessnun, a veteran bush pilot with a consuming urge to share the grandeur of his state. Within an hour we landed on the edge of a small lake, 100 miles from the nearest traffic jam, shopping center, neon sign, and—for all I know—fellow human being. Only the rustle of woodland sounds and the lap of water against the shore disturbed a peace that I have come to think of as distinctly Alaskan.

Alaska is the only state in the Union without an official nickname. But I can understand the dilemma of the phrasemakers—what catchy saying or slogan could capture the majesty of Alaska?

GILBERT M. GROSVENOR

Taxi of the North, a floatplane wings over Columbia Glacier on Prince William Sound. "Flyingest" people

Contents

in the Nation, Alaskans take to the air in work and play—to conquer the bush or to reach weekend camps.

MORE THAN ANYTHING ELSE, Alaskans like to talk about Alaska. Some reminisce nostalgically about the old days—the fading frontier past. Others voice concern over today's vexing problems—industrial development, conservation, lack of roads, native land claims. Many speak glowingly of the promise of tomorrow—a promise that for the moment centers increasingly on petroleum. And everybody talks about the *real* Alaska.

"Yes sir," shouted my sea-drenched companion as our small fishing boat labored through the heavy swells of the stormy Gulf of Alaska, "you're looking at her now—the *real* Alaska. You can feel her all around you." I nodded affirmatively, but I did not tell him that I had also heard much the same thought voiced by a fellow passenger on a Marine Highway ferry as it plied the blue serenity of the Alexander Archipelago, by a farmer in the lush Matanuska Valley as we walked among rows of crisp, green lettuce, and by a moose hunter in the shimmering yellow of an autumn forest on the Kenai Peninsula.

Weeks later in my journey through the giant of the 50 states, I stood with an Eskimo reindeer herder on Nunivak Island, off the western coast in the Bering Sea, watching his antlered charges graze the tundra in the soft glow of a subarctic sunset. "You have luck, my friend," the herdsman said, "at last you have come to the *real* Alaska." He spoke proudly, but he was not boastful, and I could not tell him that by then I had lost count of the number of people—tenderfoot cheechakos, old-timer sourdoughs, Aleuts, Indians, and Eskimos—who had advised me of similar good fortune wherever I had traveled in Alaska.

Such a regional pride, I believe, springs from the immensity of the state—a mass of geography too great for even the immense Alaskan pride to encompass as a whole. At the University of Alaska Geophysical Institute in Fairbanks I experimented with scissors and two equally scaled maps, overlaying a snipped-out Alaska on a map of the conterminous "Lower 48." The Ketchikan area ended up on the Atlantic Coast near Charleston, South Carolina, Point Barrow over the Lake of the Woods on the Canadian border, Kiska Island below the California border in Mexico, and Attu Island in the Pacific Ocean off Santa Barbara, California. You would have to patch together 21 of the smallest states "Down South" to equal Alaska's area.

The state's lakes alone cover seven million acres. Put together, they could inundate the land area of Maryland, Delaware, and the District of Columbia. Thousands of those lakes in the southeastern and south central forest teem with fish and support rich wildlife around their shores. In other areas, they dot the desolate tundra in such profusion that some cartographers give up on drawing in each one and merely mark their maps, "numerous small lakes."

To hunt with an impromptu whaling party organized while I traveled the other end of the state, I flew from Ketchikan, at the far southern end of Alaska, to Barrow, in the farthest north, across 1,400 miles of rain forest, sparsely wooded taiga, stupendous glaciers and icefields, cruelly jagged mountain peaks, and treeless tundra pocked by thousands of half-frozen lakes. I left Ketchikan in a drizzle, with the thermometer at 45° F., and arrived at my destination a few hours later to find slush ice forming in the Arctic Ocean at −11°.

Alaska truly lives up to her name—from the Aleut word *Alashka,* or Great Land. In 15 weeks of crisscrossing the 586,400-square-mile area, I found that the 49th State comprises six distinct and varied regions.

The panhandle stretches southeastward below the main block of the state's huge bulk. A land of magnificent fiords, forests, and glaciers, it *(Continued on page 14)*

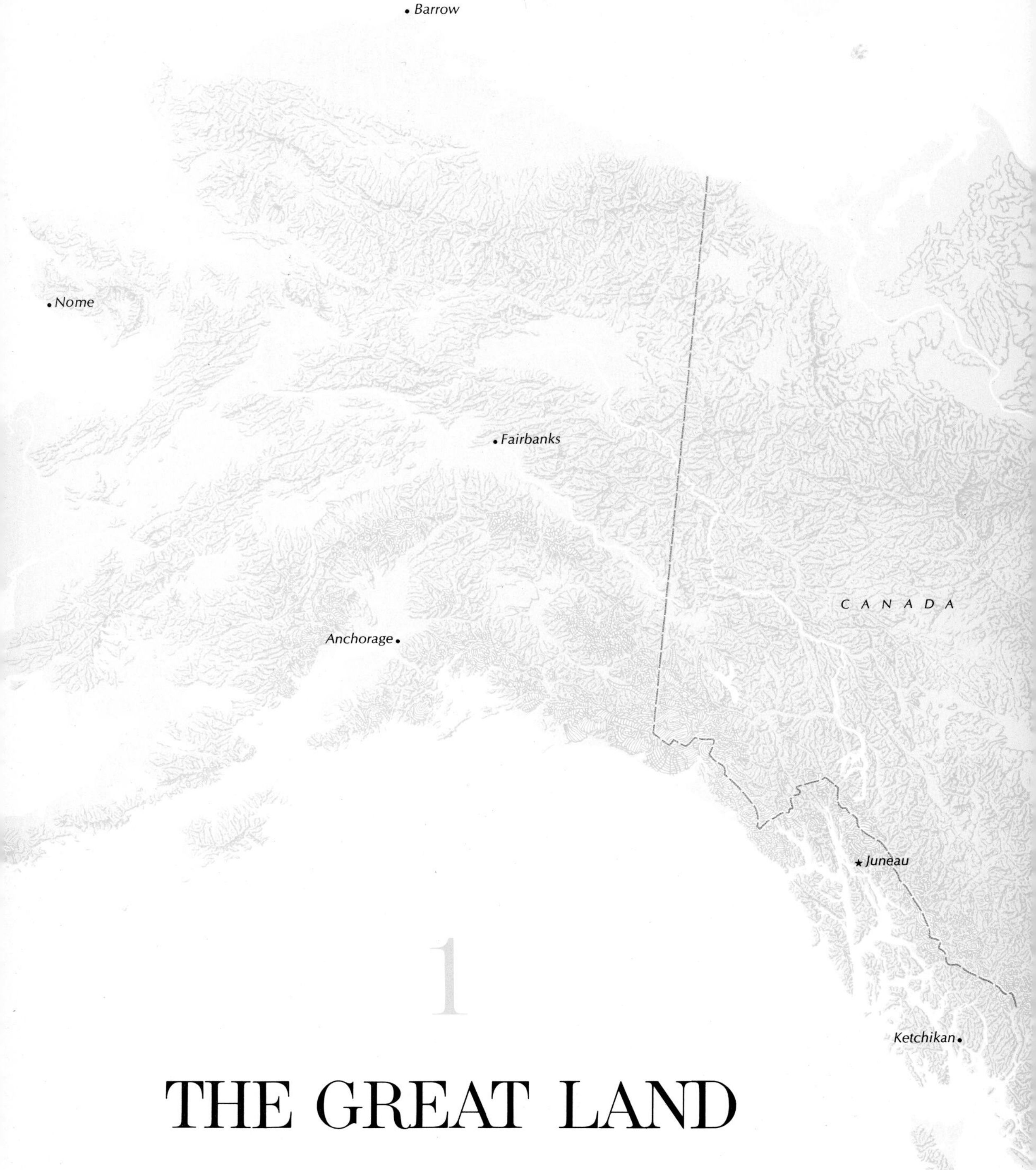

Barrow

Nome

Fairbanks

CANADA

Anchorage

Juneau

Ketchikan

1

THE GREAT LAND

Richest agricultural area in Alaska, the lush Matanuska Valley cradles more than half of the sparsely populated state's 310 farms. Sloping Chugach and Talkeetna Mountains border a 10-by-60-mile patchwork quilt of dairy and vegetable farms nestled among spruce, cottonwood, and willow. Late every summer, at the Alaska State Fair in nearby Palmer, residents exhibit their produce and livestock, including horses (right). Plans are under way for a monorail to the top of Bodenburg Butte, an 888-foot-high hump on the valley floor named for an early-day homesteader who harvested some of the lowland's first crops. An observatory and hotel planned for the top of the butte will give visitors a panoramic view.

Driving a team of eight sled dogs, contestant Rayne Redington speeds around a bend near Eagle River, north of Anchorage. In the race Redington finished first in a field of 19, covering a grueling $7\frac{1}{2}$-mile course in a record 26:05 minutes. Alaskans stage dozens of such cross-country runs as preliminary events to the world championship contests held during the Anchorage Fur Rendezvous in February. But machines, not dogs, now rank first in racing popularity in Alaska. Streaking snowmobilers (below) may reach a speed of 100 miles an hour.

N.G.S. PHOTOGRAPHERS EMORY KRISTOF AND (LEFT) GEORGE F. MOBLEY

Square-jawed lumberjack guides a grapple toward a fallen spruce near Ketchikan, southern gateway to Alaska. Salmon hauled from the choppy waters of the Alexander Archipelago (opposite) flap in the webbing of a purse seine. Previously the state's leading industries, fishing and lumbering now rank second and third behind petroleum; tourism ranks fourth.

experiences a mild, moist climate similar to that of coastal Washington or Oregon.

South central Alaska curves westward from the northern edge of the panhandle along the Gulf of Alaska to the tip of the Alaska Peninsula. Partially shielded from the intrusion of arctic air masses by the formidable Alaska Range, this area enjoys a comparatively mild climate and supports most of the state's population.

The southwest turns quickly to moorland, pointing an immensely long finger of peninsula and islands toward the Asian continent. At the collision point between the warm Pacific Ocean and the frigid Bering Sea, the area lies under a heavy blanket of fog for much of the year. Frequent storms plague the region.

The interior, lying between the Alaska Range and the Brooks Range to the north, suffers the broadest temperature extremes in Alaska. Largely tundra, much of it— with the exception of Fairbanks—remains unpopulated.

Alaska's west also lies between the great ranges, but many people consider it a distinct region. Winds from off the Bering Sea sweep across its unprotected lowland, particularly in winter months.

The arctic stretches across the top of Alaska from the Brooks Range to the sea. Its northernmost tip, Point Barrow, lies within 1,300 miles of the North Pole. A bleak monotony characterizes its inland terrain.

To sample the diversity of the Great Land, I flew 11,000 miles within the state by jet and turboprop (including one that crashed and killed all aboard a week later), by helicopter, by single-engine puddle jumper—even by a PBY Catalina. If I report that I riveted the gas tank of the first experimental PBY in Buffalo, New York, in 1933, it tells much about where good planes go when they become outdated.

On the surface I traveled hundreds of miles by snowmobile and dogsled, by freighter-ferry through the southeast's fiords and by Eskimo *(Continued on page 23)*

W. E. GARRETT AND (OPPOSITE) GEORGE F. MOBLEY, BOTH NATIONAL GEOGRAPHIC STAFF

Largest unspoiled refuge of fish and game in the country and an arena of wilderness recreation, Alaska appeals to the adventurous. In Katmai National Monument (above) an angler hip-deep in the Brooks River pulls in a king salmon; another shimmering fish vaults the falls. At left, an Alaska brown bear plods beneath an arching rainbow near Kulik Lake in Katmai. Winds of 60 miles an hour whip the lake's surface, even as sunshine dapples its shore. Below, Steller's sea lions plunge from rocky Amak Island in the Aleutians, some so startled they nearly jumped into the photographer's dory.

Overleaf: Sheer 100-foot cliffs of eroded ash, sliced by the Ukak River, rise before Mount Katolinat in Katmai. A nearby eruption in 1912 covered the area with up to 700 feet of volcanic debris.

N.G.S. PHOTOGRAPHER WINFIELD PARKS

BOB AND IRA SPRING

17

Log rafts line up outside the Ketchikan Pulp Company on Revillagigedo Island, in the Alaska panhandle. Timber contracted to the company—mostly hemlock and spruce—spreads across 800,000 acres, 90 percent of it within 8 miles of tidewater. U. S. Forest Service officials hope that reforesting in the wake of logging operations eventually will double the already mammoth stands of timber. At right, fishing boats plow the Gastineau Channel on a blue, misty day typical of southeastern Alaska. Over-harvesting in the late 1930's nearly destroyed the state's salmon industry, but strong conservation practices have begun to yield promising results; the 1968 catch totaled almost twice that of the previous year.

LINDA BARTLETT

skin boat through rapidly forming Bering Sea ice that soon would stop boat travel for the winter. I rode horses, automobiles, railroads. I crossed snowy tundra on skis and even on snowshoes, an invention that I had not worn since my boyhood at the other end of the continent in Quebec. The excruciating stiffness of hip and thigh that crippled me for the next week remains my most painful memory of the trip.

During my travels in Alaska, when my colleagues in Washington, D. C., were eating a leisurely Sunday-morning breakfast, I was still enjoying a Saturday-night frolic learning the Eskimo version of the frug at the Board of Trade Bar in Nome. For Alaska covers as many time zones as the four from Maine to California. If the Date Line had not been arbitrarily bent to accommodate Alaska, the state would spread across five zones, because a big slice of the Aleutian chain lies in the Eastern Hemisphere.

Since my return to the Lower 48, I have puzzled many of my friends by asking them to name the farthest eastern point in the United States. Many say Eastport, Maine, which technically is correct, but I then show them Pochnoi Point on Semisopochnoi Island, a fog-shrouded uninhabited rock that snuggles up to the 180th meridian from the *eastern* side, as far east as you can travel in relation to the Greenwich meridian. On the same basis, "farthest west" honors go to Amatignak Island, just 20 miles this side of the 180th meridian.

I found two great factors, climate and geographical location, influencing Alaska's present and future course.

The climate is harsh. But Alaskans become irritated by what they call the "igloo syndrome" of many outsiders who, they say, believe all Alaskans live in snow houses and eat only seal blubber. Gus Norwood, head of the Alaska Power Administration, for instance, told me over cocktails in Juneau of an immense port facility then being built at Skagway to handle silver-lead-zinc ore from Canada's nearby Yukon Territory.

"Does Skagway harbor stay ice-free all winter?" I asked.

A look of pain contorted his face. Mastering himself, he answered politely, "The only ice you'll find in any

N.G.S. PHOTOGRAPHER WINFIELD PARKS

Alaskan Pacific Coast port outside of the glaciers will be floating in your gin and tonic."

A mild exaggeration, for cake ice does form in Cook Inlet and other estuaries, but I learned later that Pacific Coast ports do indeed stay open all winter.

Pulling a National Geographic Society "Top of the World" map from his attaché case, Gus showed me that Ketchikan lies on about the same latitude as Dublin or Manchester or Hamburg; Amchitka lies no farther north than London or Brussels; even Barrow, northernmost town in the United States, occupies about the same latitude as Hammerfest, Norway, and lies hundreds of miles farther from the North Pole than the sizable mining cities on Spitsbergen.

And I must grant Gus that the temperature on Amchitka Island, in the Aleutians, has never dropped below 16° F. In Pensacola, Florida, the mercury has fallen to 7° and Nashville, Tennessee, rarely escapes 4° temperatures or lower any winter. At Kodiak, on the Gulf of Alaska, the mercury has never dropped below −12°, placing

Flames devour the Cathedral of St. Michael, a Russian Orthodox church. The century-old cathedral fell in 1966 when fire struck downtown Sitka, once a bustling fur port and capital of Russian America. Heroic townspeople braved burning timbers inside St. Michael's to rescue historic and religious relics, such as the ornate wedding crown and Gospel (above).

the first permanent Russian settlement in America on a par with Little Rock, Arkansas.

Even Gus admitted, however, that weather statistics taken from stations inland from the Pacific and Gulf of Alaska coastline and archipelago, the so-called "Banana Belt," make grimmer reading. In a single year, Fort Yukon registered 100°, four degrees higher than Miami's all-time record, and −71°. The all-time low for Alaska belongs to Prospect Creek at −80°; and the dubious distinction of all-time low for North America, at −81°, goes to Snag in the Yukon just across the border in Canada.

Deploring the outsider's belief that Alaska lies buried under great sheets of ice, Gus told me that the state's 5,000 glaciers and icefields cover only about 3 percent of the state. But even that small percentage takes in nearly 20,000 square miles of ice, including one glacier, the Malaspina near Yakutat, that stretches across an area bigger than all of Rhode Island. Only Antarctica, Greenland, and Ellesmere Island have a greater number of icefields than Alaska. And out of sight under a thin cover of earth, ice in the form of permafrost grips at least half of the rest of the state the year round. More than a quarter of the state juts above the Arctic Circle and more than half above the 60° parallel.

Rainfall records also show a wide spread, wider by far than that of any other state. Except for a brief time in summer, southeastern Alaska skies pour down almost unceasing rain. Little Port Walter, on Baranof Island, once measured 221 inches in a single year. But north of the perpetually snow-capped Alaska Range, which parallels the southern coastline and cuts off the moist ocean breezes, the interior has as little rainfall as the arid country around Phoenix, Arizona, or El Paso, Texas.

Still farther north, across the Brooks Range, the wide, barren north slope receives no more precipitation — even in the form of snow — than Yuma, Arizona, or Las Vegas, Nevada. And at the eastern end of the slope moisture barely exceeds that of Death Valley, California.

To live in a land with such wide extremes demands a tough, resourceful, and adaptable people. Such a breed wandered into the region thousands of years ago, hunting the animals that provided them with food, clothing, and shelter. Glance at the accompanying Top of the World map and you'll see the extent of the continental shelf between Asia and North America. Once this thousand-mile-wide land platform was above water, connecting the two and giving easy passage to both men and animals. Through the ages, generation after generation of hunter and hunted slowly migrated eastward. Toward the end of the last great Ice Age, the waters from melting glaciers and centuries-old snow submerged the bridge, burying all traces of these nomadic travels.

By this time, about 11,000 years ago, the resourceful hunters had established a delicate balance with nature and her creatures. As the animals migrated, the nomads followed, and where the animals grazed, the nomads built their camps.

Weathered face of Joe Kozak, a 77-year-old prospector en route to the Alaska Pioneer Home in Fairbanks, mirrors four arduous decades of digging in the gold fields of his adopted land. Kozak, a Polish immigrant, never made the big strike. Beginning in 1880, waves of gold seekers streamed through frontier settlements like Dyea (above), now abandoned to the fireweed.

Steam billows from a new fertilizer-manufacturing complex near Kenai, one manifestation of a petrochemical boom sparked by oil and gas strikes in the Cook Inlet basin. A workman (opposite) checks a maze of pipes used to convert natural gas into high-nitrogen-content ammonia and urea. The $50,000,000 plant ranks as the largest of its type in the world.

At Onion Portage, on a high bank of the Kobuk River 120 miles east of Kotzebue, archeologists from Brown University have uncovered a stratified series of ancient campsites used by countless generations of hunters. Steps in the light-brown silt descend into trenches whose walls, to the expert, are like richly illustrated pages of a book recounting the story of Alaska's early inhabitants.

Led by Douglas Anderson, a team of scientists works with shovels and wheelbarrows, patiently exposing fishing lures, combs, harpoon points of carved bone, and other artifacts—among them some of the oldest clues of man found anywhere in the interior of western Alaska. Round tags pinned to the side of one trench classify more than 50 different layers, each marking a distinct period of habitation. Mr. Anderson believes that the debris at the bottom of the trench, in the oldest layer yet uncovered, may have been left by people living at Onion Portage as early as 10,000 years ago.

The real treasure of Onion Portage lies in its wealth of razor-sharp blades of chert, each measuring about an inch long. Set as points in the end of an antler spearhead, or as cutting edges along the side of it, they would make an effective weapon.

Identical blades have been discovered around Lake Baykal in Siberia and in Japan's northern islands. This indicates to some scientists that ancient peoples of Asia coursed eastward into America long before Europe's Age of Exploration launched sailing ships westward.

Alaska's aboriginal inhabitants fall into three groups: Indians, Aleuts, and Eskimos. Together they now number 52,000. Separately, the Eskimos count for more than half of the native population in Alaska. For that matter, more Eskimos live in Alaska than in any other place in the world.

Anthropologists still debate the cultural origins of the rugged Eskimo hunters and fishermen. From some unknown source they came—possibly from the Old World, or western Canada, or the area of the Bering Strait. Eventually they migrated across the top of the world from the northeastern corner of Siberia to Greenland, along a

Gaping cavern, carved by a subglacial stream, engulfs a scientist at the terminus of a Glacier Bay ice mass, in southeastern Alaska. One of a team supported in part by the National Geographic Society, he searches for hints about warming and cooling trends in tomorrow's climate and clues to past weather conditions. At left, tributaries of a Boundary Range glacier lick between cloud-capped peaks. From each tributary, lateral moraines—deposits of rock and soil gathered from valley walls—merge to form medial moraines that stripe the stream of ice. On high mountain ranges, heavy snowfall—sometimes exceeding 100 feet in a year—nourishes thousands of such ice rivers; glaciers cover about 3 percent of Alaska.

Floatplanes rim Lake Hood, one of the world's busiest aircraft marinas, near Anchorage. Isolated by roadless wilderness, Alaskans take to the air; one of every 50 residents holds a pilot's license. More than a dozen local airlines, many of them outgrowths of bush-plane operations, serve the state. A helicopter (opposite) ruffles a snowfield near Mount McKinley.

span of some 4,000 miles of coastline. Today most of Alaska's Eskimos inhabit the western and northern coasts of the state. In my travels, I learned that they speak two major dialects: *Inupik,* the northern tongue, and *Yupik,* the southern. Both words mean "Eskimo," or "real people."

All of Alaska's "real people" are still adapting to the cultural invasion of the white man that penetrated Alaska late in the Age of Exploration. A map in the 1727 edition of *Gulliver's Travels,* which I examined in the Alaska Historical Library in Juneau, shows the land of Brobdingnag on an immense peninsula tantalizingly similar to Alaska in shape, size, and location on the northwestern tip of North America.

But the imagined land of Jonathan Swift eluded substantiation until 1741, when Vitus Bering, a Danish explorer in the naval service of Russia, approached the Alaska mainland. His expedition marked the first recorded visit by white men.

After sighting and naming Mount St. Elias from the Gulf of Alaska, Bering turned for home. Storms and scurvy haunted his ship, the *St. Peter.* Within days of safe port, he steered for land — actually an island — that he mistook for Siberia. In coastal waters, wind and tide drove his vessel across a reef into a lagoon; before the weakened crew could haul the *St. Peter* ashore, a merciless winter storm hurled it hard on the beach. Shipwrecked and ill with scurvy, Bering died on the island that today bears his name.

Survivors of the Bering expedition reached Siberia nine months later — among them a naturalist named Georg W. Steller. During his stay on Bering Island he had made extensive notes about sea lions, sea otters, seals, and sea cows, marine mammals that provided food and clothing for the stranded sailors.

The crew brought back exciting reports of luxuriously furred sea and land animals abounding in the fog-cloaked islands between Asia and America, as well as pelts to prove their claims. Within two years, a great fur quest began.

In growing numbers, hard-bitten *promyshleniki* — Siberian fur hunters — sailed toward the east, following the animals first to the Commander Islands, on to the Aleutians, then to Kodiak Island, and finally to the mainland of Alaska. But the harvest

and the profits eventually failed, for over the years the Russians hunted the animals almost to extinction.

Meanwhile, Russian activity in Alaska whetted the interest of other nations. In July 1776, the same month a congress of American rebels issued its Declaration of Independence, Capt. James Cook sailed under the ensign of Great Britain to find the Northwest Passage for King George III.

He failed in his search. So did George Vancouver, who reported to the Lords of the Admiralty in London in 1794—after three summers of sailing the waters between the Columbia River and Cook Inlet—that the Northwest Passage positively did not exist. But the charts and surveys of the two brilliant navigators remained the basis for all maps of these waters until the end of the 19th century.

In the autumn of 1860, a United States Senator contemplated the future of his country. William Henry Seward looked far off toward the northwest, where the Russians were establishing seaports, towns, and fortifications in Russian America.

"Go on," he said, "and build up your outposts all along the coast, up even to the Arctic Ocean—they will yet become the outposts of my own country—monuments of the civilization of the United States in the northwest." Seven years later Seward's prophecy was fulfilled.

As the Nation licked its Civil War wounds, word reached Seward, then Secretary of State, that Russia wished to sell its North American colony. Hurrying to draft a treaty of cession before Congress adjourned, Seward and Edouard de Stoeckl, the Russian Minister, labored with their clerks and assistants at the State Department until four in the morning of March 30, 1867. Despite grumbling by critics that "Walrussia" was worthless—a land with no animal life except perhaps for a few "wretched fish"—Congress approved the measure early that summer, and the following year appropriated $7,200,000 for the purchase of Alaska.

The date for the ceremonial transfer of ownership was set for October 18, 1867. To the beat of drums, Siberian troops stationed at Sitka—the capital of Russian America—marched up the grassy knoll in front of the Governor's house.

They stood at attention in front of a 90-foot flagpole flying the imperial standard of Russia—a two-headed black eagle on a ground of yellow—as another flourish of drums heralded the arrival of the 200-man U. S. Army contingent.

The Russian Governor, Prince Maksutov, and his attractive 22-year-old wife watched the proceedings, awaiting the striking of their sovereign's flag and the raising of the Stars and Stripes. Few of the Russian citizens of Sitka had gathered for the ceremony, for they regarded the event with great sorrow. To them the day marked the end of 126 years of tsarist exploration and rule on the North American continent.

King Island dancer in Nome wears a replica of a mask that represented ancestral ghosts to his western Eskimo forebears.

A booming salute of gunboat cannon rang out. Princess Maksutova fought back tears as the Russian flag was lowered. Suddenly, a gust of wind wrapped it around the flagpole ropes. The harder the lanyard was pulled, the more the standard refused to be struck.

Finally a man had to be lifted in a bosun's chair to cut loose the banner. Briefly, it fluttered free, and then fell onto the bayonets of the soldiers below.

Overcome by emotion, Princess Maksutova fainted. By the time her attendants revived her, the Stars and Stripes flew from the flagpole, and the Princess and other Russians in Alaska stood on the soil of the United States.

Once it had gained possession, the distant government in Washington seemingly forgot about the new purchase—so much so that the few Americans at Sitka were forced to appeal to Canada for a warship to protect them from a threatened Indian uprising. Initially, Alaska came under the jurisdiction of the Treasury Department, and for years the only federal officials in the immense area governed under the title of Collector of Customs—a far cry from present-day Alaska, where every other wage earner draws a government paycheck of some sort.

Just before the turn of the century, gold strikes on the Yukon and Klondike Rivers in Canada brought a stampede through the Alaskan ports of Skagway, Dyea, and St. Michael. When prospectors found gold on the beaches of Alaska's Seward Peninsula, 20,000 adventurers flocked to the area, and Nome became a boomtown.

But the bonanza soon failed, and Nome shrank to its present 2,500 population, most of it Eskimo. Today abandoned gold-mining dredges litter the countryside, one of them within nugget-throwing distance of the municipal airstrip.

In a continuing quest for new sources of wealth, major petrochemical companies have been extracting exploratory cores in Norton Sound near Nome. But if they do find minerals in commercial quantities, it is doubtful that the discovery would bring back the rip-roaring Nome boom days. Undersea prospecting requires heavy investments of capital and machinery, not colorful sourdoughs with their placer pans.

During the Theodore Roosevelt conservation era, enormous tracts became federal reservations of various kinds. When Alaska achieved statehood on January 3, 1959, the Federal Government still held 99.8 percent of the land.

The state has since taken over several tracts and applied for a number of others, but even so, when Walter Hickel resigned as Governor of Alaska to become Secretary of the Interior in Washington, D. C., he assumed responsibility for ten times more Alaskan landscape.

In 1912 Alaska became a proper territory with its own legislature, but the Great Land continued to doze in virtual hibernation till World War II.

Off-duty airline stewardess, whose company arranges tours through arctic Alaska, joins spectators at a performance of the King Island dance troupe.

Even before the attack on Pearl Harbor in 1941, the Nation's military leaders, alarmed by a threatening Japan, had begun to strengthen the Alaskan outpost; and once the United States entered the war, the military rushed men and planes to defend the top of the world. By mid-1943, more than 140,000 Allied troops were serving in Alaska; in that year a huge task force fought a bloody battle to wrest Attu Island, in the Aleutians, from Japanese control. The military reacted with such alarm to the Japanese thrust because Alaska sits athwart a Great Circle route between dozens of Old and New World major strategic centers.

Overleaf: Livid light of a late October sky bathes the tiny Eskimo village of Shishmaref, just 21 miles south of the Arctic Circle. Waves of the frigid Chukchi Sea lap at the shore of Sarichef Island; beyond, the coast of the Seward Peninsula curves toward the horizon.

Visiting the Aleutian island of Shemya, I noted a number of signs printed in Japanese. They puzzled me until my guide pointed out that fewer miles separated us from Japan than from Anchorage, that Tokyo itself lay only about as far away as Ketchikan. "Shemya offers the only friendly landing field for hundreds of miles between the United States and Japan, and planes flying the Great Circle route sometimes land here to adjust mechanical difficulties," he explained.

I visited the Air Force installation at Shemya with NATIONAL GEOGRAPHIC photographer George Mobley. As we waited to place a call to our headquarters in Washington, D. C., we amused ourselves with a globe and a piece of twine. We soon discovered the same length of string that spanned the distance between Shemya and our home office also reached Australia, Indonesia, South Viet Nam, Thailand, Burma, Pakistan, India, Tibet, Afghanistan, anywhere in Red China, and virtually all of Russia.

Because Alaska lies across the shortest attack routes between the Old and the New Worlds, since World War II the United States has continued to maintain a large armed force in the state. Thousands of young bachelors in the military only aggravate the long-standing imbalance of the sexes in Alaska. Statistics contradict themselves and some indicate the ratio may eventually approach an ideal fifty-fifty, but certain hints in the Alaskan culture tend to indicate that a shortage of girls persists.

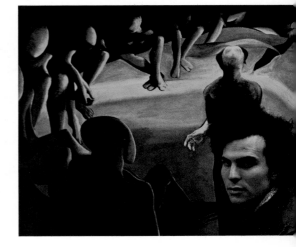

A radio commercial for an Anchorage bar, for instance, offers drinks at only 25 cents for unescorted women, and many of the general circulation publications in Alaska carry lonely-hearts columns listing girls interested in marriage.

"Japanese girls make wonderful wives. We have a large number of listings, many interesting [*sic*] in marriage," says one agency. Other agencies offer docile girls from Guadalajara, Mexico, and buxom beauties from Germany.

A sourdough friend of mine told me about a miner in the wilderness near the Brooks Range who corresponded with a girl in California through a lonely-hearts club and sent her, sight unseen, a passage to come to his cabin for a wedding in the bush. His girl lost her nerve, but her roommate, who recognized the sound of opportunity when it knocked, grabbed the ticket and went in her stead. The couple lived together 50 years and died within three weeks of each other.

The Alaskan bachelor who takes on a wife faces the job of bringing home the bacon at $1 a pound in Anchorage, nearly 20 percent more than it costs in Seattle. And the prospector on the Seward Peninsula must think long about taking a spouse if, at the end of a dogsled ride to Nome, he has to pay $1.39 for the same bacon.

Building a house costs considerably more than Down South, even in Anchorage with its wharves and freight connections with the Lower 48. At distant Barrow, construction costs jump to 3.6 times the national average. As a result, a housing shortage persists in Alaska, despite the low density of population.

Rehearsing behind a scrim, dancers of the Anchorage Civic Ballet parody The Nutcracker. *Art instructor Bill Brody (above) shows one of his paintings at the University of Alaska in Fairbanks — northernmost U.S. center of higher education. Many visitors to the state still expect cities to be backward boomtowns, a preconception that annoys Alaskans.*

But on the cheery side, wages run high in Alaska; the median income per household in Anchorage stood at nearly $14,000 in 1970.

Alaska's population density of only one per two square miles compares with 68 per square mile in the Lower 48. And one-third of the people of the state live in one small section — the greater Anchorage area.

Over expanses as large as whole states Down South, no man sets foot for years on end. Over thousands and thousands of acres, moose, brown bear, and caribou, bald eagles, horned puffins, and ptarmigan reign undisturbed.

In many parts of Alaska, man — the invader — still travels at his own peril, a fact that my friend Fred Heacock pointedly confirmed as we flew a low-level patrol of the 626-mile-long military fuel pipeline from Fairbanks, deep in the interior, to Haines, near the upper end of the panhandle.

In −16° F. weather we took off in a single-engine plane equipped with a non-functioning heater and radio. Fred explained that he had borrowed the plane because he had damaged the wings of his own while making a forced landing on the Haines Highway the day before.

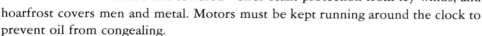

"Since we don't have a radio, we'll just have to buzz each pumping station as we go by," he said. "Someone will teletype ahead that we are coming. That way, if we crash, people will know within a very few miles where to find us."

But if the attractions are great enough, man seems willing to challenge almost any peril.

On another day at the same Fairbanks airport, I became caught up in the excitement of the rush to the north slope — scene of what may become the greatest oil find in North America. I mushed out to the plane with several investors from the midwest, headed for Sagwon to see for themselves the changes oil was bringing to Alaska's arctic, and a group of hard-bitten roustabouts going back for another turn at braving −40° F. temperatures.

Jobs for Eskimos on the drilling rigs of the north slope pay up to $18,000 annually, a prodigious wage for the impoverished Arctic. But working conditions are almost unimaginable. Around the drilling rigs, plywood shelters — roofless so the pipes can be

JEN AND DES BARTLETT

raised and lowered — offer scant protection from icy winds, and hoarfrost covers men and metal. Motors must be kept running around the clock to prevent oil from congealing.

In spite of the hardships, some experts predict that a town of 15,000 eventually will spring to life on the frigid slope. If so, it would equal the present population of Alaska's second city. Fairbanks today numbers about 15,000, roughly the same as Sikeston, Missouri, or El Reno, Oklahoma.

But by Alaska standards, a city of 15,000 becomes a metropolis. The capital at Juneau, with its 6,050 people, ranks with Siloam Springs, Arkansas. The population of the entire state does not equal that of Omaha, Nebraska.

And throughout the state, no snakes exist at all.

Snow-covered Kuskokwim River meanders across the tundra near Bethel, in western Alaska. Ice on the river freezes to a depth of several feet in midwinter. Although the subsoil remains frozen the year round, in spring the tundra becomes a spongy carpet of vegetation. Above, scarlet bearberry leaves grow from a bed of frost-covered lichens, grasses, and sedges.

   NATIONAL GEOGRAPHIC PHOTOGRAPHER GEORGE F. MOBLEY

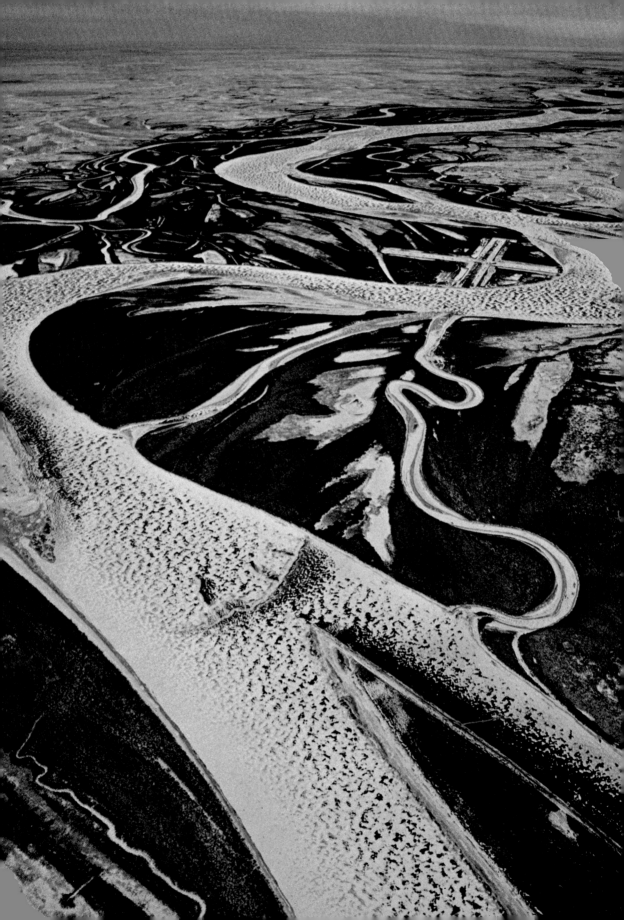

Breaking through a low overcast, my airliner from Seattle skimmed above the choppy waters of Clarence Strait on the approach to Annette Island Airport, aerial gateway to the Alaska panhandle and jetport for Ketchikan, the 49th State's southernmost city. Along the dark jade mountain slopes of the islands below me, spruce, hemlock, cedar, and alder grew in dense profusion under the benign encouragement of a soft drizzle. Logs en route to Ketchikan's 60-million-dollar pulp mill patterned the waters of the tree-lined bays and coves like giant jackstraws cast by some titan hand.

Alaska's panhandle, a 30-mile-wide strip of mainland fringed by the Alexander Archipelago, stretches for 550 miles southeastward from the state's blocky land mass. And the 16-million-acre Tongass National Forest, largest of the Nation's timber reserves, blankets virtually all the island-dotted extremity.

At Annette Island I transferred to a creaking Grumman Goose amphibian for the hop to the Ketchikan waterfront on Tongass Narrows, 20 miles to the northeast. Landing with a soft squash in a mist that to my unpracticed eye could have hidden a two-acre log raft, the pilot taxied toward shore, zigzagging and dodging among dozens of the thousand fishing boats that plow in and out of the harbor during salmon season. This first brush with Alaskan flying left the hair bristling on my neck, a reaction I did not outgrow in three months of travel with nearly a score of pilots — all of whom somehow managed to maintain an unnerving insouciance through fog, rain, hail, blizzard, and gale.

In the vastness of Alaska, aviation outranks all other forms of transport, reckoned in passenger miles. Of every 1,000 Alaskans, 20 are licensed pilots — about six times the national average. And the Federal Aviation Administration predicts the number of pilots in the 49th State will nearly double by 1985.

Ketchikan lies squeezed onto a narrow coastal slope between the Tongass Narrows and the mountains of Revillagigedo Island. Part of the business district hangs over the water on pilings. Dating from 1887, the year the first cannery opened on Ketchikan Creek, the city now boasts a population of 6,994. Founded on salmon, it still claims to be the "Salmon Capital of the World."

Ashore, Frank Seymour, then manager of the Ketchikan Chamber of Commerce, greeted me with a jovial hello and led me to his car for a drive around town. Despite the drizzle, fishermen, loggers, and visitors from Down South crowded the sidewalks, for I had arrived in late August, the simultaneous height of the area's three major harvests — salmon, timber, and tourists.

"Every summer brings more visitors than the last," Frank explained.

Ketchikan, once an insular village with more boats than cars, looks skyward to the day of the giant jets. Just across the narrows from Ketchikan on Gravina Island, work is under way on a new 10-million-dollar jet airport with a 7,500-foot runway and a new terminal.

But on the ground Ketchikan faces the harsh realities of a late-arriving automobile age that accompanied the opening, in 1954, of the huge pulp mill — one of the state's largest private employers, with a thousand people on the payroll. Newcomers arriving from the Outside brought with them the West Coast belief that life without an automobile verges on the unthinkable. Soon the city had nearly half as many cars as it had people. Then in 1963 the opening of the Marine Highway, with car ferries linking the panhandle to road systems north and south, added a new influx of autos. As a result, Ketchikan's streets, laid out long ago with a frugal regard for the value of the city's few flat acres, carry an almost intolerable burden of traffic.

CANADA

Skagway•
Haines •

Juneau ★

• Sitka

Ketchikan•

2

WHERE FIORDS
AND FOREST MEET

Observation deck offers an unobstructed view of Ketchikan's waterfront as the ferry M.V. Taku plies the Inside Passage, a marine highway that threads Canada's western coast and Alaska's island-dotted panhandle. "Five blocks long, four blocks back from the water, and two blocks up Deer Mountain," Ketchikan residents say of their city. Only energetic pedestrians use stair-stepped walkways like Wiley Street (below). Southeastern Alaska's awesome scenery—magnificent fiords, glaciers, and the Tongass National Forest that sprawls over practically all the area—draws growing numbers of tourists.

BRYAN HODGSON, NATIONAL GEOGRAPHIC STAFF (ABOVE),
AND STEVE AND DOLORES McCUTCHEON

"And I came to Alaska looking for elbow room," Frank muttered, as we circled the center of town looking for a parking place.

The prices in grocery store windows surprised me, and that same day the Alaska Agriculture Experiment Station reported that a basket of groceries costing $19.22 in Seattle would set back the Alaskan shopper $26.58. And prices for services run even higher—a fact I verified later in Anchorage by doling out $3.50 for a haircut and another $1 for a shoeshine—before tips.

Seeking shelter from the persistent rain, we ducked into the Frontier Bar for my first encounter with the Alaska saloon—an institution representing for many Alaskans the political forum, fraternal lodge, forensic arena, and recreation hall that makes tolerable the lopsided ratio of glorious but brief summers to long dreary winters of their northern homeland.

Ketchikan's Frontier Bar stands as a classic of the kind: sawdust on the floor, dark but cozy illumination, a walrus head mooning down from the wall in imbecilic solemnity, a stuffed king crab defended by the local citizens—along with 150 other king crabs in 150 other bars across the land—as the largest ever caught, polar bear and brown bear pelts, caribou antlers, and the inevitable moose rack.

Frank and I struck up a conversation with Andy Mackey, the proprietor. "I'll tell you something about Alaska," Andy said, once he learned the purpose of my visit. "See that bunch of fishermen—those tough-looking guys at the back of the room? I'll bet you that those roughnecks have more years of college behind them than half the schoolteachers in Ketchikan. Most of them play on college football teams Down South and come up to Alaska for the big money during the summer."

Although the salmon fishery had not yet recovered from severe setbacks of the past two decades, the 1968 catch had almost doubled the previous year's disastrous harvest. Frank and several eavesdropping fishermen agreed that the future looked brighter because of strong conservation practices. They doubted the state's catch would ever again reach the 900 million pounds of salmon packed in the late 1930's; the huge harvests of those years had severely depleted salmon stocks. But everybody seemed

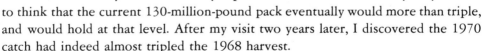

NATIONAL GEOGRAPHIC PHOTOGRAPHER GEORGE F. MOBLEY

to think that the current 130-million-pound pack eventually would more than triple, and would hold at that level. After my visit two years later, I discovered the 1970 catch had indeed almost tripled the 1968 harvest.

Frank and I went back out to find that the mist-filled overcast had rolled away in one of the lightning changes that characterize the weather of southeastern Alaska. Frank was visibly relieved. "You've arrived at the beginning of the panhandle south-easter season," he said. "From late August through December we get rain, rain, and more rain, but we may produce a few days of sunshine for you yet."

We drove to the ferry landing, and I boarded the M.V. *Malaspina* to take the now-famous trip up the Inside Passage, a route that threads through narrow channels among the forested islands of the Alexander Archipelago and extends almost the

Campers beside Ella Lake in Tongass National Forest delight in Alaska's elbow room. The U. S. Forest Service maintains 135 cabins scattered through the 16-million-acre tract for rental to visitors at about $2 a day. Above, an angler fishes for trout in Humpback Lake.

W. E. GARRETT, NATIONAL GEOGRAPHIC STAFF

Closing the ring, a skiff draws the end of a purse net toward the mother ship, a salmon-fishing boat on the sun-coppered Gulf of Esquibel, off Prince of Wales Island. A purse line will close the bottom of the seine, trapping fish inside. A net 1,500 feet long can haul in 12,000 salmon, worth about $3,000. Stacked like cordwood, frozen salmon await processing (right) in a Juneau cold-storage plant. A Ketchikan cannery worker (far right) packs roe for shipment to Japan.

length of the panhandle. Joining the early arrivals at the rail, I watched the loading of cars and campers. In the hustle-bustle, pretty young matrons worked up a rosy flush as they chased down excited children.

The scene offered a lively melodrama of vacation good spirits. But beside me two stubble-bearded old-timers in checkered shirts, faded trousers, and leather boots—each wearing a knife with a six-inch blade in its scabbard—watched the proceedings with sour expressions.

"The Governor acts right proud about this Marine Highway ferry system," said one, "but it looks to me like these boats just fill the state with riffraff."

The traffic report for fiscal 1969 showed the state's seven car ferries had carried 139,299 passengers and 38,500 vehicles. In the immensity of Alaska, even if those passengers had all come from the Outside and settled permanently, they would have boosted the population density by only one person to every four square miles. But to the two sourdoughs even a single ferryload represented a threat to their precious elbow room.

Most of the travelers planned to stop over for a day or two of sightseeing in cities along the ferry route before boarding a later ship for the next stage northward. But the best sightseeing in the panhandle—and in my opinion, virtually in the world—I found from the deck of the ferry itself. I have coasted the length of Norway and Labrador and most of the western coast of Greenland, but nowhere have I seen more magnificent fiords than along the Inside Passage of the Alexander Archipelago.

A passenger with the flat accents of the Central Plains of the Lower 48, staring goggle-eyed with me at the primeval grandeur, asked that sempiternal question posed between Americans meeting far from home.

"Where are you from?"

I told him I lived in the billiard-table-flat cottonfields of the Mississippi-Yazoo delta.

"I come from Kansas, so I guess this jumble of woods and rocks doesn't make either of us think of home much," he said. "I'd sure hate to plow and sow those hills to a crop of wheat, but whoever plants the trees around here does a bang-up job."

Totem Bight State Park exhibits reproductions of poles gathered from deserted Tlingit villages. Three poles rise before a copy of a multiple-family dwelling of the early 1800's.

Eagles coursed the shoreline, and porpoises and killer whales raced through the blue waters ahead of the ship. Pert little tugs chugged in and out of inlets, and purse seiners wallowed homeward under a full load of salmon, followed by flocks of screeching gulls. Overhead, shadows of low-hanging clouds driven by the brisk sea breeze raced across the forested slopes of majestic mountains.

Rarely in the unending cover of virgin timber did I see scars left by chain saws, for Federal regulations protect scenery along steamer lanes. An occasional small patch of clear-cut land has intruded in recent years, however, and with signing of a 50-year contract between the U. S. Forest Service and a plywood corporation for cutting 8.75 billion board feet of timber, conservationists have become alarmed that protective measures will be even more loosely enforced when heavy cutting begins. Indeed, by the time of my second visit the Sierra Club had brought a suit to hold up the contract until the Forest Service could give better guarantees of protecting the esthetic values of the southeastern forests.

Before the first organized company of American settlers crossed the Rocky Mountains into California, Russian governors at Sitka were giving glittering full-dress balls and theater parties. Sitkans traveling on the ferry assured me that much influence of Russian America remained there, so I disembarked for a layover.

AMONG THE FIRST SITKANS I met was a man who introduced himself as Father Anastassy Tsonis, an Orthodox priest. When he heard of my interest in Russian-American history, he led me to the onetime Russian boarding school, the only remaining structure of what had been the seat of the Russian Orthodox Church for all of North America. On the way he pointed to a large, empty island splitting traffic in the middle of Lincoln Street, Sitka's main thoroughfare.

"The spire and dome of the Cathedral of St. Michael stood high over the rest of Sitka from 1848 till January 2, 1966," he said. "Then it burned to the ground in less than half an hour. The National Park Service called it the finest example of Russian church architecture in the United States, so we plan to rebuild on exactly the same plan.

"If the good people of Sitka of all faiths and of no faith had not risked their lives to save the precious icons, relics, and paintings of the cathedral, I would not have much to show you. But they recklessly plunged into the flames and came out carrying what they could find in the smoke."

The old boarding school, built of clapboard-sheathed logs, serves as headquarters for the Diocese of Alaska, largest in North America of the Russian Orthodox Greek Catholic Church. The structure was erected in 1842, six years before the cathedral and probably before any other still-standing building in Alaska, though three surviving buildings in Kodiak vie for the title.

In the chapel I found a book that held between its ornately tooled covers a Gospel in Aleut and Russian on facing pages, written with the spidery Slavonic letters of the Orthodox Church's liturgical language. Alaska's first resident bishop, Innokenti, had translated the Gospel into Aleut in 1828. A man of many parts, the energetic Bishop Innokenti had also made the chairs we sat in. Their curious blend of massiveness and graceful design had stood up to more than a century of hard use with no sign of wear.

Father Anastassy also showed me the silver-and-gold-framed icon of the militant St. Michael, patron saint of the city. Most precious of all the icons of the diocese, it had been saved once from shipwreck and again from the cathedral fire. A number of other icons had been taken to Juneau for display just before I arrived, the first time they had ever been out of Sitka.

A still-strong reminder of Alaska's Russian heritage, 26 Russian Orthodox churches and 59 chapels—scattered through the panhandle, along the Gulf of Alaska, out the Aleutian chain, and up through the vast delta of the Yukon and Kuskokwim Rivers—continue to serve the spiritual needs of some 15,000 parishioners, 95 percent of native extraction.

That night I ate by candlelight at the chic Canoe Club restaurant of the Potlatch House motel. Over dinner my host, Bill Cook, who won the All-Alaska Logging Championships for three straight years, explained the techniques of overcoming competitors with intimidating names like Packsack Louie, Booger Red, Pipepole Slim, and Brooklyn Joe. Most of the 14 skills tested—among them tree climbing, tree topping, and cable splicing—remain useful to a modern *(Continued on page 55)*

Crevasses 60 to 100 feet deep score the 1½-mile-wide face of Mendenhall Glacier, ice originally deposited as snow a century ago on the 1,500-square-mile Juneau Icefield. Melt from the slowly retreating glacier feeds Mendenhall Lake, 115 feet deep in places. Swimmers (below) brave the brisk water of nearby Dredge Lake.

Cloud-fringed Mount Juneau towers over Alaska's capital. The box-like Federal Building dominates the business district fronting Gastineau Channel. Alaska's fourth largest city, Juneau sprang up in 1880 when Joe Juneau and his partner discovered gold nearby. The boom fizzled early in the 20th century, and prospectors moved to new strikes in the interior. Though fishing and lumbering remain important industries, 50 percent of the city's wage earners work for the state or Federal Government. At right, golfers play an evening round on the tailings of an abandoned gold mine. The estimated value of ore left in the residue gave the Million Dollar Golf Course its name.

NATIONAL GEOGRAPHIC PHOTOGRAPHERS GEORGE F. MOBLEY (ABOVE) AND WINFIELD PARKS

logger, unlike some rodeo events, which have evolved into crowd-pleasing stunts. The full course takes a grueling eight hours, but Bill said his 6-foot-6-inch, 220-pound frame wasn't the whole story, since his successor, Mike McGraw, stands only 5 feet 11 inches with a medium build.

"But I've turned 38 and he hasn't hit 22 yet, so I took my skills back to the logging outfit I'm with."

Bill Cook's living as a logger seems assured. Jack Culbreath of the U. S. Forest Service told me that timbering regulations now in effect should produce sustained yields far into the future.

"Because both hemlock and spruce reproduce best when exposed to full sunlight in this cool, wet climate, loggers harvest timber in clear-cut blocks rather than by thinning. In the Maybeso Experimental Forest we tested by cutting one block of a square mile to see whether natural seeding would establish a new forest. And it did.

"The Forest Service also is working to improve the value of other woodland resources, such as salmon-spawning streams. Come back next summer, and you'll see an experimental machine called the riffle sifter at work on Alaska streams."

"Riffle sifter. Now that's certainly a snappy name. How does it work?" I asked.

"On the same principle as your wife's vacuum cleaner. While your wife is interested in a dust-free carpet, we want to remove the fine silt and sand from spawning gravels. Salmon eggs develop better in clean gravel, and we hope to boost the survival rate of salmon fry from the normal 10 percent to possibly 40 to 60 percent."

Virtually all of Alaska's resources came into demand after the era of uncontrolled exploitation in the Lower 48 during the 19th century. By the time the demand for timber made it profitable to cut Alaska's forests, a sophisticated conservation policy had developed throughout the country. As a result the ax and saw have never slashed away the state's natural wealth as they did

W. E. GARRETT, NATIONAL GEOGRAPHIC STAFF

in the Lower 48, and Alaska's forests today offer a model of conservation management.

Greeted by bright sun again the following morning, I seized the chance to continue the ferry ride through the overwhelming Inside Passage, bypassing intermediate stops and riding to Skagway at the end of the line.

Skagway's false-front stores and Gay Nineties decor reminded me of the parlors of impoverished Southern gentility who stubbornly memorialize a glorious past forever gone. But there ends all relation between Skagway's past and any kind of gentility. The glorious past Skagway celebrates consisted of rowdy saloons, boisterous fancy houses, and whooping boom times of the 1897-98 Klondike gold rush.

For a few months 15,000 gold-rush boomers thronged the town, hoping to make a killing directly or indirectly from the new-found bonanzas across the cruel Chilkoot and White Passes in the Yukon Territory. However, the strike panned out for only a

Juneau Icefield dwarfs a ski-equipped Air National Guard plane supplying a research party. Working under a series of National Geographic Society grants, team leader Maynard M. Miller determined that the icefield shows evidence of growing in volume, although most glaciers spawned by the field continue to recede. Above, Dr. Miller descends into a glacial crevasse.

lucky few. The boom soon collapsed, and Skagway shrank overnight to a town of fewer than 1,000 inhabitants.

The town remains much as the gold rush left it, still rich in the lore of a half-forgotten era of American history. Today civic-minded citizens of Skagway seek to preserve the old-time flavor of their community for the benefit of growing numbers of tourists who travel through southeastern Alaska via the Marine Highway. Several nights a week during the summer, local residents stage a lively "Days of '98" show, complete with can-can girls and gambling games with make-believe money. Crowds of visitors watch the gun-blazing re-enactment of "The Shooting of Dan McGrew" that climaxes each performance.

Many residents also dress in Gay Nineties costumes during the tourist season. A flamboyantly attired man wearing a broad-brimmed black hat, frock coat, string tie, crimson vest, black trousers and boots greeted me as I disembarked. Introducing himself as Jack Kirmse, proprietor of Alaska's oldest curio shop, he invited me on an informal tour of the town.

We strolled down Skagway's board sidewalks, stopping at the Trail of '98 Museum that houses scores of interesting relics of the gold rush. We stepped into the lobby of the Golden North Hotel, built in 1898, and Jack remarked that its rooms contain authentic furnishings of the late nineties. Eventually we wound up at Skagway's venerable institution the Pack Train, which proclaims itself to be the "oldest continuously operated bar in Alaska."

The Pack Train provided headquarters for gold-rush operations of notorious confidence men and such promoters as Tex Rickard, Alex Pantages, and Philadelphia Jack O'Brien, as well as the poet of the Klondike, Robert Service. An assayer's scale for weighing gold dust still stands available for those who wish to pay their tab the old way, and a purring cash register serves the modern tourist.

As Jack and I chatted, his vest adornment caught my eye. He told me he was wearing the world's largest watch chain, a memento of a gold-rush faro dealer named Pat Renwick. Pat had commissioned Jack's father, Skagway's first jeweler, to convert ten large nuggets won at the gaming table into a suitable trophy of his prowess. During the short time left to him in his turbulent life, Pat pawned and redeemed the three-pound chain as often as two and three times daily as his fortune ebbed and flowed.

Back aboard the ferry, I watched as Skagway faded into the distance and wondered if perhaps I had seen it for the last time as the ghost of the Klondike gold rush. Nearby, construction crews were building an immense wharf to handle the silver-lead-zinc ore from the Anvil-Vangorda field in the Yukon. Such a new flood of mineral wealth from across the Canadian border could exorcise the ghosts of the Klondike days and turn Skagway into a modern boomtown with paved streets, parking meters,

Dead art form comes to life beneath the modern-day chisel of Leo Jacobs, a Port Chilkoot woodcarver. Carl Heinmiller, instrumental in reawakening the Chilkat Indians' interest in totem carving, holds a model to guide the artist. Totemic crests adorn Leo's blanket (above), made of wool and yellow cedar bark; a ravenlike clan symbol decorates his helmet.

LINDA BARTLETT

Cruising toward the head of the Inside Passage, the ferry M.V. Matanuska leaves the twin towns of Haines and Port Chilkoot behind and sails for Skagway, 17 miles up the Lynn Canal. Petroleum storage tanks (center) — the starting point of a 626-mile-long military pipeline to Fairbanks — dot the shore. Four ferries make the 1½-day run between Prince Rupert, British Columbia, and Skagway, with stops at six panhandle towns along the way. From the forward observation lounge (right) passengers view a steadily changing panorama.

BRYAN HODGSON, NATIONAL GEOGRAPHIC STAFF (ABOVE), AND NATIONAL GEOGRAPHIC PHOTOGRAPHER GEORGE F. MOBLEY

supermarkets, plastic-and-chromium cocktail lounges advertised by neon moose heads over the doors, and only an annual costume pageant left to celebrate the receding memory of the olden days.

Many of the 463 citizens of Haines, a 17-mile ride back down the Inside Passage from Skagway, work at sawmills and at piers loading timber aboard Japan-bound freighters. Most visitors to Haines travel the short distance to Port Chilkoot, where Chilkat Indians perform their ceremonial dances. Some of the women weave blankets dyed black with alder bark, yellow with lichen, blue-green with copper ore, and the men carve masks and totem poles.

Originally an artifact of the Northwest Pacific Coast Indians, the totem pole served as a public document to record important events for a people who had no written language. Gradually, as smallpox and tuberculosis took their toll of the Indian population and more and more tribesmen sought work in salmon canneries, the totems fell into disuse, until the art of carving them—and even the ability to interpret them—threatened to disappear.

Credit for reviving interest in the Northwest Indian arts must be passed around to many anthropologists, artists, and historians. But the credit for perhaps the most practical venture must go to Carl Heinmiller, a World War II veteran who lost an eye and three fingers fighting alongside native commandos from Fiji. He came to Alaska to form a cooperative that bought the U. S. Army's Fort William H. Seward —lock, stock, and barracks.

Finding the Indians apathetic about their past, he set about restoring racial pride by first learning and then teaching the almost-vanished arts. Today the Chilkats show justified respect for the creative carving and weaving skills of their ancestors. Young and old alike join in perfor-

NATIONAL GEOGRAPHIC PHOTOGRAPHER WINFIELD PARKS

mances of ritual dances, much to the delight of the ferry-loads of visitors who flock to witness the revival in tribal self-esteem.

At the Heinmiller home, once quarters for officers of the Fort Seward garrison, Mrs. Heinmiller announced that Carl was stranded in Juneau by bad flying weather. Checking my watch, I discovered I could just catch the ferry and ride through the storm in a cozy stateroom to meet him at Juneau in the morning. But Carl, conscious that he was failing to keep an appointment with me in Haines, stayed alert for the first rift in the stormy skies and flew home. So we passed each other "like ships in the night," a frequent accident in Alaska, where I sometimes thought the best way to make contact would be to station myself in an airport—any airport—and interview the restless Alaskans as they came and went on their endless aerial voyaging.

At Juneau, I expected to be greeted by an old friend, Mike Miller of the Alaska

Old-timers swap gossip on the main street of Petersburg, a fishing and logging town on Mitkof Island. Many long-time citizens of Alaska disapprove of the urbanization currently transforming areas of their state. False-front buildings flank Skagway's Broadway (above); new industry may soon dilute the days-of-'98 gold-rush flavor the town seeks to perpetuate.

Spirited dash for the finish line ends the choker-setting competition, one of 14 events in the All-Alaska Logging Championships held each July in Sitka. In this match, contestants drag 1¹/₈-inch cables about 50 feet to a 5-foot spruce log, pass the chokers around the log, fasten them, and return to the starting line. Winning times average less than two minutes. In the field, the men would then winch the log to a nearby road or watercourse for transport to a lumber mill. Loggers at the two-day tournament also compete in chopping, sawing, and tree climbing—skills learned while working in the area's $50-million-a-year timber industry. At right, high-pressure water jets peel bark from logs in a Sitka pulp mill. Japanese capital helps finance both pulp and lumbering operations in Alaska's panhandle.

Travel Division. But I scanned the faces of the waiting crowd in vain till I tentatively approached a bearded fellow with a worried look.

"Mike?"

"Hah, at last!" he bellowed in relief, recognizing me by my voice. "But what happened to your magnificent moustache?"

"And when did you grow a beard?" I countered.

After a brief exchange of tonsorial histories, Mike told me of the excitement he still feels at each ferry arrival: "Imagine an area larger than Kentucky with a half-dozen fair-size cities, including the state capital, and only about 290 miles of roads. And none of those between towns. When the *Malaspina* made the first trip late in February 1963, every person in town not bedridden by incurable disease turned out for its 10 p.m. arrival. We thought the wharf might collapse. Then the great ship loomed out of the fog with all lights blazing, flags flying, horns blasting. The outside world had come to our doorstep. We all wanted to cry—and some did."

JUNEAU'S PAST ISOLATION makes it all the more incredible that the little city has successfully resisted demands of Alaskans farther north to move the capital nearer the state's geographic and population centers. Its 6,050 citizens still fear that upstate pressure may force the state's offices to move to Anchorage or Fairbanks, a disastrous prospect for Juneau because government is the town's chief industry, ranking above lumbering or fishing. The huge Federal Building dominates the business district, and half of the city's breadwinners cash a state or federal check.

Under the onset of autumn rains and diminishing hours of daylight, most tourist activities had ended for the year. Even the most ardent buffs had abandoned the only golf course in southeastern Alaska, a nine-hole affair laid out on the barren, grassless tailings of the played-out Alaska-Juneau Gold Mine.

And to the east on the nearby icy heights of the Boundary Range, winter weather had already forced closing of the camps where the noted glaciologist Maynard M. Miller has annually studied the changing health of a score of glaciers under a series of National Geographic Society research grants. But on Juneau's coastal strip only the faint nip of the mountain breeze hinted that the edge of North America's fifth-largest icefield lay just ten miles inland.

Taking me on a short drive to the Mendenhall Glacier, Mike explained that glaciers form in the high mountains when winter snowfalls exceed the summer melt. Most years 100 feet or more of snow fall on the great Juneau Icefield, packing down into 1,500 square miles of ice hundreds of feet deep. The enormous weight of that ice mass pushes 16 major and many smaller glaciers, or ice rivers, down the mountain slopes, but usually at a pace measurable only by surveying instruments. Snow that fell on the upper Mendenhall the year that the United States purchased Alaska from Russia is just now approaching the 1½-mile-wide, 200-foot-deep ice face.

The Mendenhall Glacier stretches 12 miles from the perennial winter of the icefield to the maritime climate at the face. Typical of most of southeastern Alaska's receding glaciers, it has oscillated in a slowly retreating pattern since the mid-18th century, exposing about 70 feet of lateral ground each year. Soil and rock deposited by the glacier some 200 years ago lie about a mile and a half from the present face.

In vivid contrast, the much larger Taku Glacier—draining southward into Taku Inlet about 40 miles east of Juneau—has advanced more than six miles since the beginning of this century. So, according to Dr. Miller, the Juneau Icefield as a whole is actually growing in volume.

Mike showed me the gradual invasion of plant life into the uncovered terrain in front of the Mendenhall ice, and I learned that the succession from hardy primitive plants like lupine and fireweed to a young forest of spruce and hemlock takes about 100 years. The Mendenhall retreat offers a living laboratory for scientists to study what happened to a major portion of North America at the end of the last Ice Age, more than 10,000 years ago. And at the same time, the Taku advance provides an exciting opportunity to study the processes of reglaciation.

Across the Mendenhall face lies a melt pool, a lake of water milky from the rock dust ground by the ponderous glacier in its forward passage. Miniature icebergs dot the surface of the lake.

Mike gathered a few chunks of glacier ice.

"Far superior to commercial ice for cooling drinks or picnic boxes," he said. "Each chunk contains thousands of small interlocking crystals. Pressure has squeezed most of the air out of them, so the ice melts much more slowly than the larger-crystaled manufactured variety."

When the Juneau gold miners left for the Klondike rush in 1897, Mendenhall Lake did not exist, and the Taku had hardly started its resurgence. The site of the handsome Mendenhall Visitor Center, exposed in 1941, still lay deep beneath the ice.

NATIONAL GEOGRAPHIC PHOTOGRAPHER WINFIELD PARKS

At the center, staffed by the Forest Service, Mike and I sipped coffee and took turns at a telescope watching mountain goats graze on the red-gray cliffs above the glacier.

"A new resurgence could begin, even in the near future," Mike said. "If it does, the glacier could carry away this visitor center and everything before it, possibly all the way to the sea four and a half miles away. My house lies right in the way. But it took perhaps 10,000 years to retreat this far, so I figure I have time to make evacuation plans.

"When you fly to Anchorage this afternoon," he went on, "you'll view what I consider to be the world's greatest display of icefields and glaciers available to ordinary tourists. Alaska has more square miles of glaciers than the rest of the inhabited world put together, and you'll be able to get a good look at most of them from your plane."

Waning sunlight silhouettes a Russian cemetery and a reconstructed blockhouse near Sitka, called New Archangel by its founders. Such forts rimmed the town in the early 1800's when settlers fought off bloody attacks by the local Tlingit Indians.

The afternoon flight—the canny traveler takes a window seat on the starboard side going north—crossed Glacier Bay National Monument and, beyond Yakutat Bay, coasted beside mighty Malaspina Glacier and ice-sheathed Mount St. Elias, past Guyot and Bering Glaciers oozing down from the vast Bagley Icefield, Columbia Glacier dumping thousands of tons of ice daily into Prince William Sound, and Portage Glacier, calving huge bergs into its melt lake.

Before such stupendous and hostile beauty, man becomes a temporary and insignificant intruder on events far beyond his control or comprehension.

Overleaf: Tangle of ice-rimmed harbor islands shelters Sitka, scene on October 18, 1867, of the ceremony transferring Alaska from Russia to the United States. Although cake ice occasionally forms in southern harbors and inlets, panhandle ports remain open the year round.

MY ANCHORAGE-BOUND JETLINER banked in a lazy figure-eight holding pattern painfully familiar to travelers in the crowded Lower 48. I wondered what had happened, for it seemed a bit too much to be held up by traffic congestion over Cordova Airfield, a forest-rimmed strip serving a town of 2,500. Then the captain's voice sounded over the cabin loudspeakers: "Sorry, folks, but we won't be able to land at Cordova today. Another aircraft collided with a moose on the runway, and it will take some time to clear the tangle." With that we swung across Prince William Sound, and I leaned back in my seat, feeling better about Alaska, knowing that moose congestion and not air traffic had caused the wave-off.

Booming Anchorage sprawls across a broad alluvial plain at the head of Cook Inlet, midway between the northern tips of the panhandle and the Alaska Peninsula. The flat-roofed buildings of the city's business district stud the buckle of the state's "Banana Belt" — so named by veterans of 60-below winters of the interior and the arctic who regard the climate of southern Alaska as verging on the tropical. Protected from numbing polar winds by the towering mountains of the Alaska Range and warmed by the Pacific's Kuroshio Current, the south central region fairly basks in weather similar to that of upper New England. Only occasionally do Anchorage winter nights bring temperatures colder than −20° F., and seldom does the summer sun push the thermometer past the 75° mark.

Already more than one-third of the state's population of 302,173 lives in the greater Anchorage area, and newcomers and outlanders continue to pour in. A few loners, who came to Alaska to get away from it all, still hide out in the bush. Such recluses have become increasingly rare, although during my visit one old sourdough living near Mount McKinley put a .30-06 bullet through a helicopter for intruding on his "private" air. Most Alaskans, however, prove themselves to be as gregarious as any people on earth. They pile into the city and pack themselves into housing developments as crowded as any on Long Island, remaining nonetheless outspoken in their praise of the vast unspoiled wilderness that Alaska offers.

Founded in 1915 and still a village of 3,500 a quarter century later, Anchorage exploded in the forties and fifties and zoomed past Ketchikan, Juneau, and Fairbanks to become the state's largest city. "The 1970 census shows a population of 48,029, more than three times that of Fairbanks," Maurice Oaksmith, director of the Alaska census, said. "Another 76,500 people live within the greater Anchorage area."

Anchorage's mushroom growth should have suffered a sharp setback if not a death-blow on Good Friday, March 27, 1964, when the most severe earthquake recorded in North America during this century struck south central Alaska. The quake killed 114 persons, and 50,000 square miles of land heaved or sank to new levels. Earthquake-spawned seismic sea waves drowned 12 persons in far-off Crescent City, California. Even the Gulf of Mexico on the other side of the continent tossed up six-foot waves in reaction to the earth's writhing, and the level of water wells fluctuated in Florida and Puerto Rico.

Bob Reeve, one of the state's most famous bush pilots and aviation pioneers, well remembers the earthquake. It took him on one of the wildest flights of his hair-raising career.

"I had joined friends at the Petroleum Club on the 15th floor of the Anchorage-Westward Hotel prior to going home to my 62d birthday party that night," Bob recounted. "Suddenly the building began to sway 20 feet in either direction, throwing me off my stool and across the room. My watch fell out of my pocket, and I wasted minutes trying to catch it as it slid past. The elevators had quit, so we had

CANADA

Anchorage

Kenai
Peninsula

Seward

3

METROPOLIS
IN THE MAKING

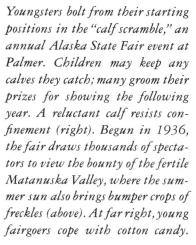

Youngsters bolt from their starting positions in the "calf scramble," an annual Alaska State Fair event at Palmer. Children may keep any calves they catch; many groom their prizes for showing the following year. A reluctant calf resists confinement (right). Begun in 1936, the fair draws thousands of spectators to view the bounty of the fertile Matanuska Valley, where the summer sun also brings bumper crops of freckles (above). At far right, young fairgoers cope with cotton candy.

to walk down 15 floors, feeling our way along and smashing in jammed fire doors.

"Now some of my enemies have spread the word that I was scared that day, a base canard I indignantly deny. But on the way down, I did pass four *other* fellows who definitely were scared."

When the people of south central Alaska steadied themselves and assessed the damage, they found they had lost more than 311 million dollars in property and untold millions in a severely disrupted economy. The land had been permanently altered, leaving some wharves underwater and others high and dry.

In Anchorage, one side of Fourth Avenue — the nearest thing the city has to a main street — had sunk 11 feet in a jumble of wreckage. Cracks gaped in the sides of high-rise buildings. Landslides carried away rail lines leading into town. Highways buckled, and bridges collapsed.

A transient people with few roots — as Alaskans are popularly regarded — should have surveyed the ruins and left for greener pastures, or at least for pastures less given to the shakes. But, determined, the people dug in, cleaned away the rubble, rebuilt the vanished buildings, constructed new piers, repaired the roads, and went back to their jobs. By the time of my initial visit, four years after the quake, few vestiges of it remained.

After a few days in Anchorage I rented a car and drove to Palmer, 43 miles to the northeast in the Matanuska Valley, hoping to find Alaska's principal farming area in full harvest. First homesteaded in 1915, the Matanuska Valley drew nationwide attention during the Great Depression when the Federal Government assisted 202 midwestern farm families in starting new lives as pioneers on the Alaskan frontier.

Roland Snodgrass, director of agriculture for the state's Department of Natural Resources, drove me through the valley. Hip-roofed barns dominating tidy farmsteads reminded me of Minnesota's dairy country. "Fourteen of the original families of the Alaska Rural Rehabilitation Corporation colonization project remain," Roland told me. "Throughout the valley, 44 full-time and 70 part-time farmers work the land. Dairy products continue to be the major income-producers, but vegetable crops — including potatoes — may soon compete with them for dollar earnings with the introduction of improved storage facilities."

N.G.S. PHOTOGRAPHER GEORGE F. MOBLEY (ABOVE AND OPPOSITE)

We stopped beside a field of superb lettuce — great firm heads colored the tender green of the first willow buds of spring. As an amateur gardener of some skill, I stood awed by the quality of the produce. Roland heard my exclamations of admiration, and a puzzled frown wrinkled his face.

Waves of barley fall before the combine of Kenneth R. Condict, an Oklahoman who settled in the Matanuska Valley in 1958. Oats and barley represent the valley's prime grain crops. Several farmers compete in growing giant cabbages (above); a 72-pounder set a record in 1968.

Overleaf: Booming Anchorage sprawls toward the Chugach Mountains, whose snowy peaks herald the coming of winter. A tent city in 1915, Anchorage exploded in population in the forties and fifties. More than one-third of the state's 302,173 people live nearby.

JOSEPH S. RYCHETNIK

"The farmer has already cleared this field of good stuff. His pickers left these heads to be plowed under for green manure."

I had to go into the field then, pull up a few heads, heft them, and peel back the outer leaves to munch a sample. The leaf parted between my teeth with the soft snap of a chilled sliver of butter. The flavor surpassed — I am forced to admit it — any lettuce I have ever grown. And to think that those hundreds of heads were destined to decay underground!

"Because of the sun's low angle, its light must pass through much more atmosphere and arrives at our fields weak in ultraviolet rays," Roland said. "We believe that this filtering action, together with the long hours of sunlight, explains the low fiber content of our leafy vegetables. It makes them tasty and succulent, but harder to ship than hummingbird eggs; you can bruise them with a dirty look."

We drove past a garden growing gigantic cabbage heads planted several feet apart.

JOSEPH S. RYCHETNIK

"Those famous 60-pound cabbages from the Matanuska Valley grow in pampered little plots like this," my escort explained. "Maybe a dozen farmers compete to grow the biggest one each year, just for fun, but the rivalry gets pretty keen. This fall, Ray Rebarchek grew two 70-pounders to take the world's record, and darned if Max Sherrod didn't show up later with a 72-pounder to take it back."

Across the road from the forcing plot grew a field of fine cabbage heads averaging the normal 3 pounds. "Outside of his hobby garden, any Matanuska Valley farmer in his right mind tries for big production of small cabbages," Roland said. "What does a housewife do with a 72-pound cabbage — make cole slaw for the kiddies' snack?"

For years farmers planted only safe cereals, grasses, root crops, and hardy leaf vegetables. Recently, however, they have begun to experiment with more tender crops like corn and tomatoes — in fast-maturing varieties, of course, for the Matanuska Valley has only a 108-day growing season. Before leaving, I sneaked a few seeds of the "polar variety" tomato to dazzle my gardening competitors back home with the first fruits of the season.

On the drive back to Anchorage, beside the road I saw a wizened Indian about 5 feet tall, wearing a white ten-gallon hat, a Navy captain's four-striped full-dress coat, and a jaunty goatee. He accepted my offer of a ride, with impressive dignity.

Bill Ezi, 70-year-old chief of a 50-man village of Tanaina Indians, an Athapaskan-speaking people, had inadvertently left his new rifle at a hotel in Anchorage the night before and was hastening to reclaim it.

"Plenty good rifle," he said. "Big rifle, .30-caliber. For years I use a single-shot .22. Big rifle better for moose and bear."

I expressed horror at the idea of using even a semi-automatic .22-caliber rifle for

Dressed in an angel costume, Denise Butcher shouts encouragement to her husky on Fourth Avenue in a children's event at the Anchorage Fur Rendezvous — called the "Mardi Gras of the North." Alaska's biggest get-together of the year, the festival takes place each February. Above, a tense contestant awaits the starter's gun in a championship dogsled race.

NATIONAL GEOGRAPHIC PHOTOGRAPHER EMORY KRISTOF

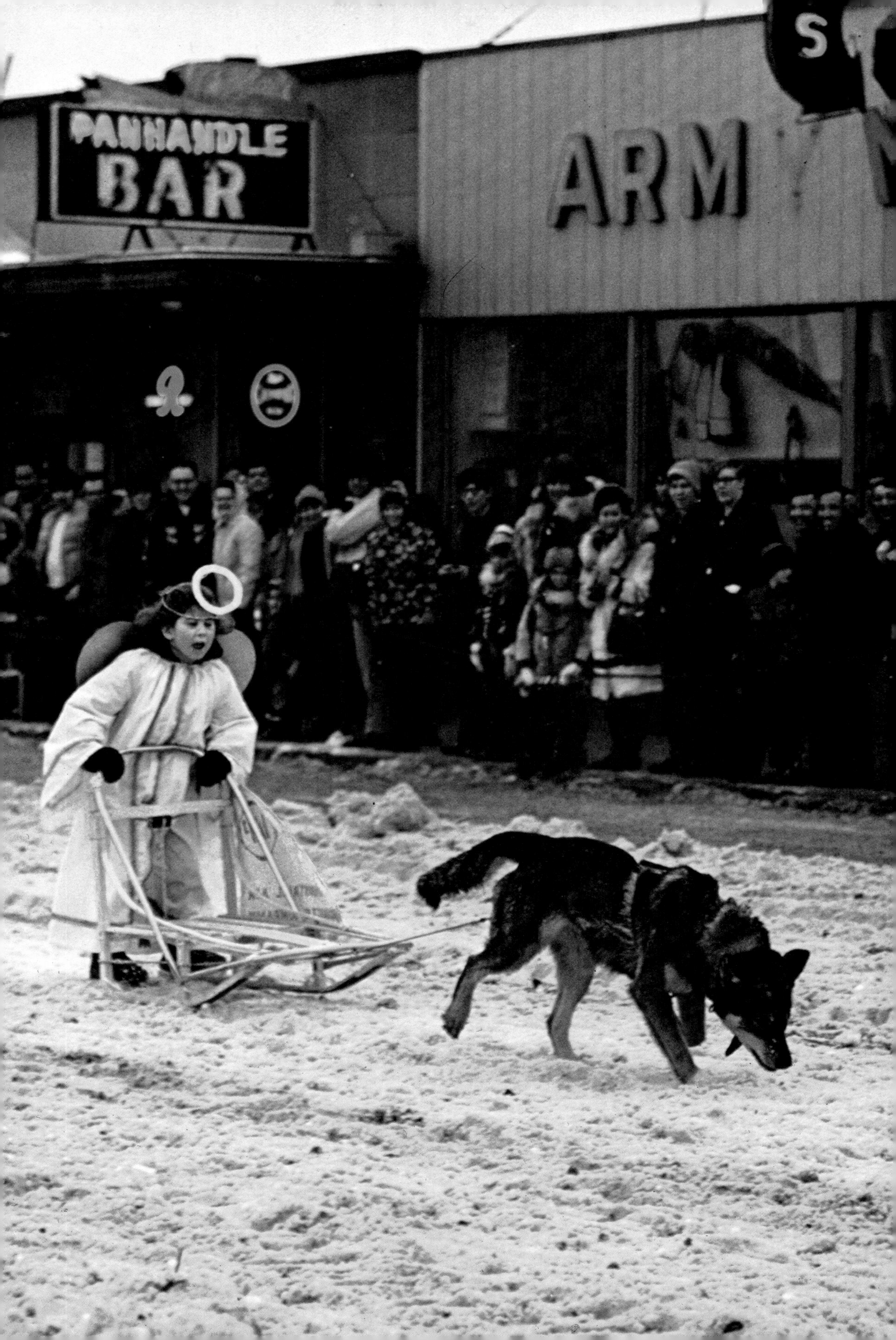
PANHANDLE
BAR
ARM

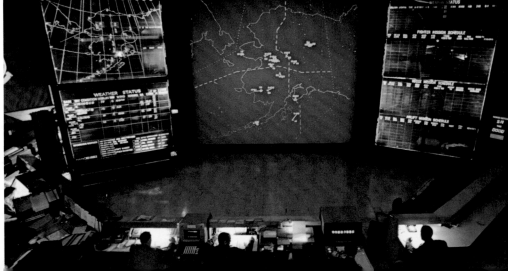

Sun's last rays glint on Nike missiles poised on Mount Gordon Lyon in the Chugach Mountains northeast of Anchorage, base for 125 soldiers of the North American Air Defense Command. Alaska's strategic location near the top of the world underscores its role in the continent's defense system; the state lies athwart the shortest attack routes between the Old World and the New. In the NORAD Regional Combat Center at Elmendorf Air Force Base (left), headquarters of the Alaska radar network, display boards flash the status of far-flung forces. The computer-controlled center panel plots aircraft operating over the state. When maintenance needs shut down the computer, technicians use the manual board at top left. Other panels record weather conditions and report reconnaissance and airlift missions.

shooting big game, much less a single-shot, but Chief Bill pooh-poohed the danger.

"I shoot moose or bear in the lung. He jump a little like fly bite him, but he don't even know I shoot him. He just mosey along till he drop, and he still don't know I shoot him."

I regarded Chief Bill with considerable respect. He cannot weigh more than 120 pounds, so I asked him how he packed moose haunches in from the kill.

"I keep strong dancing."

"What kind of dance—Indian, or rock and roll?"

"What's the difference? You dance one, you dancing the other."

As Chief Bill disembarked at his modest lodgings, he thanked me and then jerked his thumb at the imposing Anchorage-Westward Hotel.

"When I am a boy, I shoot plenty animal where hotel stand. Hotel stink up hunting. Everywhere in Anchorage no good for hunting no more."

That evening I dined 15 stories above Chief Bill's old hunting grounds with Lyman Woodman, a retired Air Force officer who now works at the U. S. Army's Alaska headquarters at nearby Fort Richardson.

Casualty of Viet Nam fighting, a young soldier, homeward bound, sips a cup of coffee in the passenger terminal at Elmendorf Air Force Base.

"Quite a view, don't you think?" Lyman remarked as we waited to be seated. It was indeed. To the east Anchorage fanned out against the cloud-draped backdrop of the Chugach Mountains. To the southwest, in Cook Inlet, huge, floodlit oil production platforms, built to withstand 30-foot tides and one of the world's strongest currents, cast an eerie glow on the chilly waters.

While we ate, a subtle shift of air currents slowly lifted the cloud cover to the north, and Mount McKinley—rising 20,320 feet into the sky—loomed into view, 130 miles away.

The setting sun slowly turned the snowy crests from pink to peach to scarlet and then to deep purple. Just before North America's mightiest mountain faded into the night, a formation of delta-wing jet interceptors streaked across its face. To Lyman the view had suddenly become deeply symbolic.

"Now you're looking at the *real* Alaska," he said. "The military presence makes Alaska. Every third man working in the state is in uniform, and about half of the remaining labor force, directly or indirectly, is part of the Government. The situation will hardly change, either, for Alaska almost touches Asia and offers an enormous shield against attack from the Old World on the heartland of the New World."

At Lyman's invitation, a few days later I went to Fort Richardson—almost a part of the city—for a joint air-ground, live-fire exercise.

With Col. Kenneth E. Dohleman, commanding officer of the 172d Infantry Brigade (Mechanized) and members of his staff, I sat on a knoll overlooking a cleared lane called the Bowling Alley. About 1,500 yards away, a stock of jalopy carcasses represented an enemy bunker. In the forest to the right lurked Bravo Company of the 5th Battalion of the 23d Infantry and a platoon of tanks. Farther back, 4.2-inch mortar and 105-mm. howitzer crews stood by to provide artillery support.

The attack opened with dive-bomb, rocket, and napalm attacks by pilots of the Air National Guard's 178th Tactical Fighter Group from Springfield, Ohio, flying F-84F Thunderstreaks. The planes had seen their best days, but the weekend warriors laid their charges across the pile of junked cars like full-time professionals.

Mortar shells pasted the old cars, 105-mm. shells threw scraps of torn metal about, and gunfire from the tanks tore jagged holes in the tangle of jalopies. Then the soldiers of Bravo Company moved out from the woods into the open field, and swept over the enemy strongpoint. The battle ended with nobody hurt in spite of the number of men involved and a terrifying exhibition of firepower.

That night I went to the flight line at Elmendorf Air Force Base to greet soldiers returning from more serious conflicts. Many of the sick and wounded from our Far East military operations come home through Elmendorf on C-141 StarLifters, and the landing at Anchorage gives most of them the first sight of the States in many months. I rode the short distance to the flight line in a bus with five service wives, part of a group of Red Cross volunteers who come out many times a week at all hours of the day and night to greet the men.

The plane taxied to a stop, and 29 ambulatory patients burst out the doorway into the cold, whooping and throwing snowballs in the sheer excitement of being back in their own country. Bulky casts on arms and torsos caused many overcoats to gape open to the wind, but the youngsters seemed to welcome the frosty bite of the air of home after the hothouse atmosphere of their tropic duty. They piled into the bus and trundled away to a nearby snack bar to fill up on good wholesome hamburgers and ketchup.

The volunteers and I boarded the plane to wait on the 28 litter patients. Swiftly the Red Cross ladies passed out hot chocolate, newspapers, magazines, and snacks. They chatted with the men and jokingly quelled friendly arguments between prostrate soldiers. Many patients touchingly offered to pay for the magazines and chocolate.

Remembering the destructiveness of the firepower demonstration, I felt a pinch at my heart to hear a pink-cheeked boy who had just been through the real thing wistfully ask if the Red Cross perhaps had brought a piece of bubble gum. The wise and experienced ladies had indeed brought it, and we left the youngster chewing happily.

Riding into town after watching the evacuation plane depart and breakfasting with the off-duty flight crew, Lyman and I passed two handsome office buildings joined by a mall.

C-141 StarLifter descends toward Elmendorf loaded with wounded servicemen. The base handles some 900 such flights in a 30-day period.

"Those belong to the Tyonek Indians," Lyman said. "In all the tangle of native land claims and cries of disaster threatening the aborigines, the Tyonek story makes good telling. Let's call on their lawyer, Stanley McCutcheon."

Before the big oil strike of 1957 in Cook Inlet and along the Kenai Peninsula, Stanley said, the Tyonek Indians lived in utter squalor.

"Inadequate" hardly described their housing, he told us.

"In a village of 200 people, 30 'night walkers' volunteered to stay up while others slept because there was not enough bedding space to go around. But suddenly, with the discovery of oil nearby, the Tyoneks' Moquawkie Reservation on the western shore of Cook Inlet became valuable, sought-after land."

In the legal battle that followed, the Tyoneks eventually consented to let the

Federal Government lease their reservation to interested oil and gas firms, provided that all money from such options would revert to the tribe. In this way the Tyoneks gained full control of their finances.

With the $12 million received from the sale of the leases, the Tyoneks rebuilt their village. Today its modern homes fronting on neatly laid out streets stand as a model of what Alaska's native people can accomplish, given the opportunity and the wherewithal to do for themselves.

But the Tyoneks did not stop there. Once they had built their own homes, they purchased controlling interest in a small construction company and put their young men to work as apprentices in the building trades.

With Tyonek financing the firm—Braund, Inc.—grew rapidly. In late 1968 the company was supervising the construction of 300 homes for indigent Eskimos in Bethel on the Kuskokwim River, and young Eskimos were learning to wield hammer and saw under the helpful guidance of Tyonek tutors.

BRYAN HODGSON, NATIONAL GEOGRAPHIC STAFF

The next day I headed into the country once again, drawn by the vivid yellow autumn foliage that garbed the lower slopes of the Chugach Mountains. Retracing my route up the Matanuska Valley, I turned eastward toward Glennallen and a link-up with the Richardson Highway, then south toward the port town of Valdez. I drove through the Indian log village of Copper Center, deep into game-rich alpine forests, up over the backbone of the Chugach Range at Thompson Pass, and down past Bridal Veil and Horsetail Falls.

At the end of the road, old Valdez lies in ruins. Abandoned buildings lean at precarious angles, mute testimony that the town lay closest of any to the epicenter of the Good Friday earthquake. Geologists warned the citizens against rebuilding amid the devastation because the soil structure might one day send their homes sliding into the sea. So the townspeople decided to move to a rock-ribbed site four miles away. There, founded on sheer determination and an abiding confidence in the future, a new Valdez rises.

I spent the night at Valdez and next morning drove to the ferry landing to board the M.V. *Chilkat* for a trip across Prince William Sound to Whittier, southeast of Anchorage on the Kenai Peninsula. Early-morning mists had made the boarding ramp slippery, and a tall, powerfully built man picking his way along the incline lost his footing and fell with a sharp crash. Several of us ran to help him up, but he put up his hand to forestall us.

"Just let me lie here and take the count of nine," he said.

I recognized the craggy features of Muktuk Marston, possibly the best-known living sourdough, and one of the founders of the Alaska Territorial Guard during World War II. After a breather, Muktuk—few know him by his real first name of Marvin— let us help him to his feet. As an old horseman I have hit the ground with a bone-snapping shock often enough to recognize the stance of a man with freshly broken

Windows gaping, an abandoned hotel testifies to the force of the 1964 earthquake and the seismic sea waves that followed. Residents of Valdez, closest town to the quake's epicenter, moved to a more stable site four miles away. At Homer, where land subsided from 4 to 6 feet, the name of a beached fishing boat echoes the spirit behind disaster recovery efforts.

 NATIONAL GEOGRAPHIC PHOTOGRAPHER WINFIELD PARKS

NATIONAL GEOGRAPHIC PHOTOGRAPHER WINFIELD PARKS

Tyonek, the Indian village that oil built, nuzzles the shore of Cook Inlet. With the discovery of oil near their reservation in 1957, residents of the then-squalid village of 200 hired lawyers to advise them. The Tyoneks agreed to lease their land to the oil companies but insisted that all money received from options be turned over to the tribe. The Indians built modern homes for themselves (left), invested in a construction company that employs their young men, and pledged to help other Alaskan native groups improve their standard of living. At far left, Tyonek children—freed from poverty that once haunted their village—frolic in the snow.

ribs. That bowed back, forward-sloping shoulders, and shallow breathing told the story which X-rays later confirmed—four ribs had given way. But a few broken ribs scarcely checked the flow of narrative from one of Alaska's great raconteurs. As we stood down the channel headed for the open sound, he recounted some of his Alaskan adventures.

"I got the name Muktuk at Point Hope during the war. I had done 65 miles behind the dogs in below-zero weather, and a hospitable Eskimo invited me into his hut. We sat, stripped to the waist, telling stories and eating *muktuk*—whale skin and blubber—brought to us by a charming Eskimo maiden. After devouring a few pounds I stood up to stretch, and my host asked eagerly if I had finished eating. I realized then that unknowingly I had been in an eating contest with a champion. So I said I was merely waiting for him to bring out the mustard to go with the main course, now that we had finished the appetizers. He conceded defeat and put the name of Muktuk on me. It has stuck ever since."

MUKTUK TOLD of his part in organizing the Eskimos into a "tundra army" in the grim days of 1941 to help scout the vast emptiness of mainland Alaska and the Aleutian chain, guarding against Japanese intrusion.

"Everyone wanted a part of the action," he said. "I had to tell an 84-year-old Eskimo that his legs couldn't stand up to scout duty. Having informed me that he didn't know what he needed legs for since he had no intention of running from anybody, the old fellow picked up his rifle and put a shot through a tin can at 200 yards. I signed him on the spot.

"To head the scout unit in Koyuk, a village on Norton Sound, I swore in Sgt. M. Penigio—a schoolteacher acquaintance of mine and without a doubt the best shot around. The sergeant ran a sharp unit and kept good records.

"Everything went well until I dismissed a certain captain who had been sent up to help out at my headquarters in Nome. He went back and tattled to the Regular Army that the M in Sergeant Penigio's name stood not for Michael, but Margaret, and I lost a good sergeant."

The ferry turned into Columbia Bay, and we crept up on the 2½-mile-wide face of Columbia Glacier. Capt. Richard Hofstad came down from the pilothouse to chat.

"The ice stands 200 feet above the water and reaches to the bottom, 75 fathoms down, so that makes a wall of ice 650 feet high. Columbia is second only to Malaspina as the largest tidewater glacier in North America, and it drops 40 miles and 12,000 feet from the mother icefields at the foot of Mount Witherspoon."

A chill wind blew off the ice. Newly calved bergs floating by cracked and snapped like musketry drill as stress patterns shifted in reaction to the sudden freedom from the awful pressure they had endured for centuries.

"The glacier moves an average of 4.1 feet a day," the captain said. "But this time of year, it moves more like 7 to 10 feet. A berg could calve any second now. Here, let me see if I can help it along."

He blew long blasts on the ship's whistle. With a roar and rolling crash like summer thunder, tons of ice slid down the glacier's face, plunged deep into the water, and bobbed to the surface again, sending out concentric rings of waves. The ferry rocked tipsily as the waves hit us, and ice cakes banged against the hull.

The entire run to Whittier, on the Kenai Peninsula, passes through magnificent scenery, but after the Columbia Glacier the rest seemed tame. At Whittier motorists from the ferry drive their automobiles aboard railroad flatcars and ride through two tunnels to the main highway at Portage. Here the other travelers turned north to return to Anchorage, but I headed south down the east coast toward Seward.

Southern terminus of the 470-mile-long Alaska Railroad that runs inland to Fairbanks, Seward gave early promise of becoming the state's principal metropolis. But the railroad moved its headquarters to Anchorage, the military built a fuel-handling pier at Whittier and a pipeline from Fairbanks to Haines, Anchorage lured deep-draught vessels with new port facilities, and Seward's promise withered.

Then came the Good Friday earthquake, and in minutes an already ailing city suffered more damage measured in dollars per capita than any other port in the earthquake zone. The Federal Reconstruction and Development Planning Commission set commercial port damages at $15,375,000.

Years after the 1964 disaster, the citizens talk about the earthquake interminably, repeating for the thousandth time what they were doing when the first tremor struck, how they fought the disastrous waterfront fire when storage tanks burst and burning oil poured into the harbor, and how a huge seismic sea wave picked up an 80-ton locomotive and hurled it like a giant cannonball into the city's public works building.

Hundreds looked over the damage, gave up, and moved away. But 1,800 stubborn people refused to leave the mountains and glaciers, the fiords and lakes, the moose, bear, and mountain goats of their scenic peninsula.

A few wait wistfully for the return of the sea-rail commerce that once made Seward, but more realistic citizens look to the mountains behind them. With Patrick Alvarez, then manager of the Seward Branch of the First National Bank of Anchorage, I sought to survey the nearby wilderness kingdom that may restore Seward's health.

We enlisted the aid of Alex Rule, a fine-arts teacher at the high school, to pilot us into the back country. Once aloft, our plane skimmed below the snow line down narrow valleys densely populated by brown and black bears that fled from the noise of our passage. On the seemingly sheer vertical

LINDA BARTLETT

Whimsical sign welcomes visitors to Portage, a tiny crossroads village on the highway linking Anchorage with the Kenai Peninsula. The scenic peninsula soon may become a mecca for tourists.

face of every razorback ridge in those tremendous mountains, herds of mountain goats and Dall sheep somehow found a foothold and grazed on invisible pasturage.

A snow flurry caught us in a narrow valley, and we lost our horizon. With grim rocks towering over us on both sides, we suffered a few tense moments before breaking through the mouth of a pass leading to the Harding Icefield, spawner of Lowell, Bear, and Chernof Glaciers.

The mountains of Alaska have the sharp sawtooth ridges and fissured sides of young ranges newly pushed up from the earth, but Harding Icefield shows that the process of aging moves rapidly at those frosty heights. Rock *(Continued on page 93)*

Overleaf: With a crash and a roar, 200-foot-high Hubbard Glacier calves a berg into Disenchantment Bay near Yakutat. Waves soon rocked the small boat. Ferry captains sometimes thrill passengers by attempting to trigger calving with blasts of the ships' whistles.

STEVE AND DOLORES McCUTCHEON

Flare of burning gas illuminates the Monopod, a one-legged oil-drilling and production platform of two oil companies, Union and Marathon, in the Cook Inlet basin. Twin derricks of a Texaco-operated platform rise in the background. Eight oil companies operate year round from 14 permanent offshore platforms engineered to withstand 4-foot-thick ice floes borne by the inlet's swift tidal currents. Submerged pipelines carry the crude to shore for loading onto tankers and shipment to southern refineries. Each platform can drill from 30 to 32 wells. Escaping dross (right) silhouettes workers on Atlantic Richfield's King Salmon platform. Natural gas from nearby Kenai Peninsula wells provides heat for many Alaska homes.

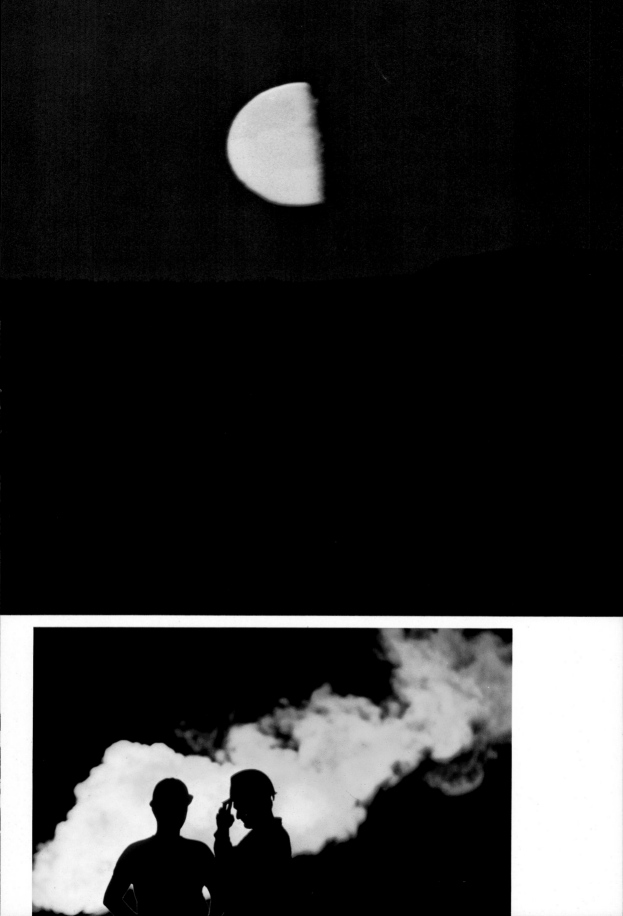

fragments cracked off the slopes by frost soon pepper even the latest snowfall, and small landslides stain the fresh snowcaps of the highest peaks. The work of pulverizing the young sierra down to a chain of softly rounded old hills, like the Laurentians or Appalachians, proceeds apace—visible to the most transient visitor.

But even the most furious pace of erosion cannot reduce the wild grandeur of the Kenai Mountains for ages to come, and Seward plans to profit from that wilderness beauty. At Lost Lake high in an alpine valley the water stays frozen into June, and the snow lasts on the slopes till July—a sharp contrast to sea-level Seward 10 miles away, where the temperature rarely falls to zero even in winter. Young businessmen of Seward have turned their backs on the railroad and look to the hills instead, hoping to open a ski resort some day to capitalize on the superb gifts nature has given the area.

Meanwhile, a band of Massachusetts scallop fishermen, discouraged by depletion of East Coast beds, came to Seward to try their hand at dragging the bottom for new beds. They were electrified to find huge scallops in startling quantities in their trawls. On their first commercial cruise, they hauled in six times the biggest load they had taken in decades of fishing back home.

When I talked to the fishing captains of the four scallop boats, they told me they pay their 14-man crews roughly $2,000 each at the end of each 13-day cruise. Pat Alvarez confirmed that income tax withholdings are based on a $40,000 annual income estimate for each fisherman.

Heading back toward Anchorage, I decided to cut across the rugged peninsula to Kenai. Here civic leaders have abandoned the wilderness for the modern technology of the petrochemical industry. Many oil companies are developing a major gas and oil strike on land just outside the town and in Cook Inlet beyond the Kenai waterfront. During my visit I saw drilling crews working around the clock atop 14 huge offshore platforms capable of drilling from 30 to 32 wells each.

NATIONAL GEOGRAPHIC PHOTOGRAPHER GEORGE F. MOBLEY

North of town the petrochemical industry has built a 57-million-dollar plant to compress natural gas to a liquid for shipment to Japanese power plants. Nearby are an 11-million-dollar oil refinery, a 20-million-dollar refinery for processing crude the state receives as royalties instead of cash, and a 50-million-dollar plant for making ammonia and urea fertilizer from natural gas.

"Everybody is excited about that north slope oil," then City Manager Ormond Robbins told me.

"But Kenai dominates the only really producing area in the state, and this little city already ranks as the biggest port in Alaska with 27 percent of the tonnage handled as compared with Anchorage's 25 percent."

Since airline distance from Kenai back to Anchorage measures only 60 miles, many oil and gas employees commute by personal plane, charter, or the seven scheduled Wien Airlines F-27 and eight Alaska Aeronautical Twin Otter flights. But I

Skiers take to the trails at Alyeska, Alaska's only year-round ski resort. Scene of several major competitions—including the 1963 Olympic trials—the 2,450-foot drop and 1.6-mile run descend to only 240 feet above sea level. A jumper (above) heads for a tumble.

drove the 160 miles by highway to stop over at Alyeska Resort, the best-known skiing area in Alaska, just 40 miles southeast of Anchorage.

I arrived at the ski lodge to find people scurrying about like ants in a plowed-up nest. A bulldozer operating not far from the lodge had just gone out of control, sliding half a mile down the steep mountainside at 50 miles an hour and crashing into a building housing the lift machinery.

With the opening of the ski season three days away, Chris von Imhof, German-born manager of the resort, hurried to the scene to assess the damage. Fortunately, no one had been hurt, the driver had jumped free in time, and the bulldozer had miraculously missed the intricate lift machinery.

Probably the lowest major ski run in the world, the Alyeska main trail drops from 2,450 feet to only 240 feet above sea level. But even at that low level the top half rises above timberline for clear runs.

The resort offers far more than just good skiing. It has dogsleds for hire, drawn by real Alaskan huskies, a large outdoor pool for swimmers and sunbathers, and a 60-acre "moose pasture" where guests can hotrod around on rented snowmobiles.

IN THE DINING ROOM I met François de Gunzburg, French co-owner of the resort. "When we opened the slope in 1959, skiers showed up in old-fashioned baggy pants and skis without sharpened edges, and everyone had to keep his eyes open for moose and bear on the trails," he said. "Now, however, the fashions and the ski equipment match anything you'll find at St. Moritz, and the wildlife has left for quieter climes.

"We've had some fine competitions here — the 1963 U. S. National Championships and the Olympic trials, and soon the 1969 Junior Nationals. But the most fun comes during the International Airlines Ski Races. The event dates back to our first year of operation when the Scandinavian Airlines crews on the polar route challenged the Air France people. Now 400 skiers representing more than 30 airlines, including some from behind the Iron Curtain, compete here every winter."

I scarcely heard the last words, for a stunningly beautiful red-haired girl joined our table. Introduced as Mrs. Chris von Imhof, she turned out to be the daughter of Frank Whaley, a famous bush pilot and good friend. And, quite understandably, she also turned out to be a former Miss Alaska.

She wore a heavy parka and mukluks, hopeful of finding enough snow to work out her dog team for the first time that season, and she invited me to come along. Not since I had left Quebec in my distant boyhood had I felt the thrill of riding the runners behind an eager team that yapped with excitement at feeling the bite of fresh snow.

Later that day Chris took me to the top of the lift to the fast, powdery intermediate ski runs, and even offered to have a pilot fly me to the glaciers where skiers in the winter start a 12-mile sweep to the valley, or in summer practice their skills on the perpetual snow.

But I had to leave, reluctantly, and I could only hope the road home would lead again through Alyeska when the snow had crept down to lower and tamer slopes not quite so challenging to a middle-aged ski enthusiast like me.

Miss Alaska of 1963, Mrs. Chris von Imhof praises Toyon, the lead Siberian husky of her dog team. Far from resenting his duties, Toyon begs to be harnessed the first time that season by lifting a paw — a gesture visitors often mistake for an offer to shake hands.

Kiska

Amchitka

Atka

4   WESTWARD

PLANNING MY TRAVELS through southwestern Alaska, I wondered where I should begin. Perhaps in Katmai National Monument country on the 475-mile-long Alaska Peninsula, or on Connecticut-size Kodiak Island, across the Shelikof Strait from Katmai. Or should I start on the island of Attu, 100-odd miles from the Date Line at the end of the 1,100-mile-long Aleutian chain, and work my way eastward? I decided, finally, to begin at historic Kodiak, headquarters for Alaska's growing king crab industry.

A bustling community with a business district that looks like a newly opened shopping center, Kodiak seems somewhat miscast as the state's oldest surviving non-native settlement. But it is, and no sooner had I arrived than I found a host of citizens ready to defend their town against any claims to priority emanating from an "Ivan-come-lately" Sitka.

One staunch defender pointed out the recently restored Erskine House, built in 1794. "Baranov lived there for ten years before going on to found Sitka in 1804," he said. "Few people realize that Kodiak goes back to the time of George Washington," said another. He was right. As Washington began his fourth—and, he thought then, his final—year as President in May of 1792, the sounds of axes biting into spruce already echoed along the timbered shores of Chiniak Bay. Aleksandr Baranov had arrived from Three Saints Bay, near what is now Old Harbor, intent on building a new headquarters colony for Russia's far-ranging Alaska fur-trading operations.

Baranov had first viewed the site of present-day Kodiak the previous fall, during a trip up the eastern coast of Kodiak Island. Then in April 1792 an earthquake and accompanying seismic sea wave nearly washed away the Three Saints Bay colony.

TO TOMORROW

Spurred into action, he gave orders to move the entire village to Chiniak Bay.

One hundred seventy-two years later similar waves churned up by the Good Friday earthquake drowned much of downtown Kodiak in 30 feet of water, wreaking havoc later assessed at $22,300,000. In the rebuilding, Kodiak acquired a new harbor for small boats and a modern business district where crooked streets had long plagued motorists. But some links with the town's colonial past remain, and on street corners elderly Koniag Eskimos with Russian surnames stop to chat with each other in a Russian dialect little changed since Baranov's time.

When I arrived at Kodiak I found the nation's third most important fishing fleet — in terms of the value of its catch — tied up in the sheltered harbor because of a raging storm in the dangerous Gulf of Alaska. I had planned to cruise with the fleet and gorge on a few freshly caught king crabs out of the hundred million pounds captured in Alaska during an average year, but the storm forced me to settle for the catch of the day before. I dined, however, with Guy Powell, a highly regarded king crab research biologist of the state's Department of Fish and Game.

Protected by an insulated rubber suit, Guy has swum hundreds of miles through the icy depths where king crabs lurk, to study their reproductive and feeding habits. The Alaskan king crab industry puttered along with small catches and marginal profits till after 1950. During the next 16 years the catch rose from 1.5 million pounds to 159.2 million. But by 1968 it had fallen sharply to 85 million pounds. And, for that reason, Guy continues to brave the discomforts of his underwater research so that eventually he will be able to establish scientifically the maximum sustained annual yield Alaskans can count on.

After dinner Guy projected underwater films he has directed since 1967 showing the strange migratory habits of the king crab. Each year adults travel from shallow to deeper waters and back again. Juveniles move in what Guy has chosen to call pods, heaps of crabs 15 feet across and 6 feet deep. The pods roll across the ocean floor with each crab taking its turn feeding on the bottom or riding the top. These living mounds creep along at an astonishingly rapid rate, flowing over boulders and rocky outcroppings like a great protean amoeba from a science-fiction horror movie.

"The adults don't usually bunch up like the youngsters," Guy said, "but they do congregate in large schools. I once saw a reeflike aggregation of large juveniles 2 feet deep and a mile long. There must have been a million crabs in that one pile."

I arranged to go with Dick Hensel, then manager of the Kodiak National Wildlife Refuge, to his 2,800-square-mile domain covering the southwestern two-thirds of the island. We went to David Henley's airport to charter a plane, but because we needed a multi-engine craft to cope with the violent air turbulence, we had to wait for several

STEVE AND DOLORES McCUTCHEON

hours. A Koniag Eskimo fisherman from an outlying village, flush with earnings from the island's ten-million-dollar salmon run, had chartered the only available twin-engine plane to pick him up and bring him to town to buy a sack of groceries.

Almost immediately after we crossed the coastal mountains beyond the town, we began to see game. Bears have the curious habit of stepping precisely in each other's footsteps, so that along the ridgetops bear trails looked like the dotted lines that mark time zones on road maps. Depressions—some of them 18 inches deep, Dick told me—had been worn into the rocky ground. Tens of thousands of the great beasts must have padded down those crests to leave so deep a trace, each stepping faithfully in the same track as his father before him.

At Karluk Lake on the southwest end of Kodiak Island, half a million salmon spawn each year, and only sport fishermen or bears may catch them. The salmon-spawning beds not only provide food for about 120 bears around the 12-by-2-mile lake, but they also support one of Alaska's major fisheries.

We landed on Olga Bay—almost as far southwest as you can fly over the island—and taxied ashore beside the rotting pilings of an abandoned cannery where a party of hunters had set up camp. In a warehouse we found nine hides pegged out and salted.

"The 'square' of the pelts—that is, half the total of the length and width—used to run at least 10 feet. These average only about 7 feet, 6 inches," Dick said. "An unlimited number of bear hunters has shot 2½ feet off the size of the trophy brownies. Just because the Kodiak has the worldwide reputation of being the biggest grizzly in the world, he is being shot back to just a medium-size fellow.

Two-year-old Alaskan king crabs crowd together for protection from predators. Above, fishermen hoist a trap a-crawl with the crustaceans. King crabs may weigh as much as 25 pounds, stretching 5 feet from tip to tip. Dwindling crops following a record $44.4-million catch in 1966 stimulated urgent research to determine a maximum sustained yield.

Home from the sea, Kodiak-based fishing boats loom over a boy pacing their quiet pier. Huge waves churned up by the 1964 earthquake inundated much of the city's downtown area and damaged or destroyed most of the vessels tied up in St. Paul's Harbor, but now business booms once more. A spray-dashed crab fisherman (below) ranges far out the Aleutian chain in quest of ocean bounty—Alaska's major product after petroleum and gas. The clash of the warm Kuroshio Current with the icy flow of the Bering Sea nurtures teeming crops of salmon, crab, and halibut.

LUCKY STAR

TAMMY

GEORGE W.

"But did you see the number of families around Karluk? If we would allow only 60 bears to be taken a year instead of the present 210 or so, and give the bears five years to recover, they'd stand every inch as tall as when the Koniags hunted them with bone-tipped spears."

Dick ridiculed the stories published in outdoor magazines about the ferocity and gargantuan size of the bears in his charge.

"Certainly, they grow bigger than any other land carnivore—with the possible exception of polar bears. It depends on how you measure, but the largest we weighed went 1,375 pounds. Bears very wisely bug out the instant they suspect the presence of a human being. Sometimes a poor misguided bear will walk toward a hunter, standing up now and then to peer about because the wind is blowing from the wrong direction and he can't figure out who has intruded into his territory. Excitable hunters invariably interpret his harmless curiosity as a vicious charge. But the instant the bear spots a man, he runs for the hills and safety."

At Brooks Camp, deep within the 4,360-square-mile Katmai National Monument on the Alaska Peninsula, bears seemingly have adopted a "live-and-let-live" attitude as far as man's intrusion into their domain is concerned. With my host, Ray Petersen—like Bob Reeve, a bush pilot turned airline official —I watched from the lodge porch as a group of anglers along the banks of the Brooks River whipped the stream for rainbow trout. The anglers had spaced themselves at intervals about 200 yards apart—except at every fourth or fifth post. But these posts were hardly vacant; at each of them a big fat bear presided over his own patch of fishing ground.

JOSEPH S. RYCHETNIK

Archbishop John of Chicago (left) officiates at Orthodox Church in America rites at Kodiak in 1970 canonizing Father Herman, a Russian missionary-monk. The casket contains relics of the saint, revered for his work among natives.

The tens of thousands of salmon spawning on the river's gravel bottom had turned flaming red and passed their peak as game fish, but the bears didn't mind. They waded into the shallow stream, poked their heads underwater, and walked about "snorkeling." A swift slash of a paw usually meant a bear had caught a fish, and then with his catch between his jaws he would waddle slowly toward the bank. There, sitting like a paunchy old burgomaster, he would hold the fish in one paw and delicately pick it apart with the other.

Why the bears used such a fussy gourmet approach, I could not figure out, because they finally ate all of the fish but the jawbones anyhow. A flock of gray jays proved much more bothersome to the anglers than did the bears. Singing *"Whiskey Jack . . . Whiskey Jack,"* they persisted in perching on the tips of the fly rods. Not even the most violent shaking and cursing would send them on their way.

"Those bears seem pretty tame, but we don't advise anyone to try to push his luck with them," said Ray, whose company, Wien Consolidated Airlines, runs the monument's lodging and trout fishing concession. "Half-tame is not enough when you're dealing with brutes as big as brownies."

I recalled a story told to me by Vance Hitt, an old sourdough who now lives in

Seward. Like many sourdoughs, Vance has a native gift for storytelling, and he had held me entranced for hours with tales of his days as a prospector and miner in the Poorman district of the Yukon valley.

"In the spring of 1946 a bush pilot reported that Ed Odergard's cabin near Poorman looked deserted, and took Marshal Frank Worth in to investigate. Finding only an empty, blood-spattered cabin, they left a native boy behind and toured the district to pick up six of us miners for a coroner's jury.

"When we got back, the Indian boy had found a human jawbone, part of a skull, and Ed's overalls with his watch still in the pocket. Later, on the edges of the cabin door we discovered the telltale hairs of a brown bear.

"Ed had already planted his potatoes and put up his mosquito net, so the attack had to have taken place just a few days before. From the blood in the cabin, we figured Ed was living and probably fighting back when the bear got him."

I protested to Vance that half a dozen Alaskans had assured me bears run from human beings and several people had even encouraged me to ramble the wild country freely, so long as I made enough noise to frighten the bears away.

"Ordinarily bears won't attack you," Vance said, "but that's a mighty hungry country around Poorman, and even a rabbit might take a chunk out of you after a hard winter."

Twenty-one miles up a winding road from Brooks Camp, the scenic beauty that marks much of the monument area gives way to the awesome spectacle of the Valley of Ten Thousand Smokes, shorn of life by the cataclysmic Katmai explosion of June 6, 1912. After five days of earthquake activity that sent most of the people living in the northern part of the Alaska Peninsula fleeing to safety, Katmai Volcano, at the head of the valley, suddenly erupted. Great clouds of vapor, white-hot ash, and dust spewed skyward. Out of a vent later named Novarupta—and possibly from others as well—boiled a massive ash flow. The seething river of incandescent sandlike material poured over a 42-square-mile area to a depth of 700 feet or more in places, sterilizing the land. The accompanying hot winds that swept down the mountainsides carbonized forests for miles around.

Tlingit Indian and Russian heritage marks the ruddy features of flowing-haired Jake Amuknuk.

Ash, dust, and pumice filled the air. Kodiak, 100 miles away, reported snowlike drifts up to 12 feet deep; roofs collapsed, and the town was evacuated. In 60 hours more than 7 cubic miles of debris from the explosion rose high into the stratosphere to be carried by winds around the northern half of the world. The ash's filtering of the sun's rays caused the average temperature of the hemisphere for the year to drop 1.6° F., and gave the world some of its most brilliant sunsets since the explosion in 1883 of Krakatau Volcano in Indonesia.

Sometime during those 60 hours, the top of Mount Katmai—6 miles from Novarupta—collapsed, and a lake eventually formed in its 2-by-3-mile caldera. But precisely what caused Katmai to collapse continues to puzzle many volcanologists.

Some scientists believe that Novarupta felled its giant neighbor by siphoning off the magma under Katmai through a subterranean conduit; others question the conduit theory, contending that lava also poured from other vents at various stages of the eruption.

In 1916, leading the third of seven National Geographic Society expeditions into the area, Dr. Robert F. Griggs discovered the still-fuming valley, "full of hundreds,

Wary Alaska brown bear and her cubs rear up on their hind legs, alerted to possible danger by the quiet click of a camera. The trio stared quizzically at NATIONAL GEO-GRAPHIC *assistant editor W.E. Garrett for a moment, then turned and ran into the dense brush of their Kodiak Island home. The largest carnivores to walk the earth, brown bears may grow to 1,200 times their 1-pound weight at birth; adults like the huge snoozer at right may exceed a height of 7 feet when standing erect. Normally vegetarians, bears turn fishermen when the salmon begin to run in the autumn. Below, a cub heads shoreward with his catch, well rewarded for his white-water ducking.*

W. E. GARRETT, NATIONAL GEOGRAPHIC STAFF (OPPOSITE); NATIONAL GEOGRAPHIC PHOTOGRAPHER
WINFIELD PARKS (ABOVE); AND LEONARD RUE, ANNAN PHOTO FEATURES

no thousands—literally, tens of thousands—of smokes curling up from its fissured floor." Two years later, largely as a result of Griggs's expeditions, the valley and volcanic peaks and a vast area surrounding them became the Katmai National Monument. Subsequent additions to protect wildlife—especially the brown bear—and to include offshore islands have made the monument the second-largest reserve in the national park system, after Glacier Bay National Monument.

I sat on a knoll overlooking the foot of the valley, a glossy mass of compacted ash that looked for all the world like a cyclopean cake frosted with pink icing. Although a few fumaroles puff occasionally, seemingly in relation to volcanic activity, Dr. Griggs's ten thousand smokes spout no more. The temperature of the valley has dropped, no longer affecting watercourses beneath the surface.

Below me, Windy and Knife Creeks and the Lethe and Ukak Rivers had cut harsh, winding channels, leaving gullies and carved-out banks to relieve the blandness. Cloud shadows chased across the quiet pastel plain.

The same macabre fascination that the lifeless surface of the moon exerts on man drew me down the mile-and-a-half path to the desolate floor. Walking soon became difficult, like trudging through deep sand, and the bleakness of the landscape left me ill at ease. Except for the familiar sky above, it seemed as if I were treading on some distant planet. Turning back, I came across a fellow explorer—a wandering moose—and I felt better; even in this grim valley the eternal quest of nature to fill an ecological vacuum with life goes on.

That evening Ray flew me across the park to Grosvenor Camp, following a zigzag route so that I could take in some of the myriad sights of the park. The presence of the National Geographic Society since the discovery of the area shows in a number of the park's place names—Grosvenor Camp and Lake Grosvenor, named for Gilbert H. Grosvenor, Editor of the NATIONAL GEOGRAPHIC for 55 years and President of the Society from 1920 to 1954; Mount Griggs, named for Dr. Griggs; Mount La Gorce, named for John Oliver La Gorce, who served the Society for 54 years and suc-

LINDA BARTLETT

ceeded Dr. Grosvenor as President and Editor; Lake Coville, named for Frederick V. Coville, chairman of the Society's Research Committee from 1912 to 1937; Gruening Overlook, one of the many areas that the state's former Governor and Senator, Ernest Gruening, visited while preparing an article for the NATIONAL GEOGRAPHIC; and Geographic Harbor, named for the Society itself.

On the mudflat delta of Hardscrabble Creek we flew low over half a dozen bear families, sows with as many as three cubs. The mothers stood erect in fighting stance as if to bat us out of the sky, but the cubs frisked about, excited by the novelty.

At the camp a short stream draining Lake Coville gurgled *(Continued on page 112)*

Hook-jawed male guards his mate in a gravel nest as bright sockeye salmon fulfill their destiny. Schools may range the Pacific for 1,200 miles or more before homing in on their native waters. Returning from the sea, they battle upstream (top right) to spawn where they once hatched; nuptial colors of a chum salmon (bottom right) fade as the completed life cycle ends.

NATIONAL GEOGRAPHIC PHOTOGRAPHER ROBERT F. SISSON
(OPPOSITE AND UPPER RIGHT)

107

Sulfurous gases and steam clouds boil from the vent of glacier-wrapped Mount Martin in Katmai National Monument. Most active volcanic unit in the national park system, the monument encompasses the center of one of history's great convulsions. A 1912 eruption spewed ash as far as Washington State, shredded clothes on lines a hundred miles away, but, amazingly, killed no one. From a new vent, Novarupta, incandescent pumice flowed down the valley in a glowing avalanche. Woodland pickets (right), killed by hot mudflows, spike the pale plain. The string of 40-odd active volcanoes that stretches along the Aleutian Range forms part of the earth's most volatile seismic zone — the Pacific Ocean's "ring of fire."

W. E. GARRETT, NATIONAL GEOGRAPHIC STAFF (ABOVE), AND NATIONAL GEOGRAPHIC PHOTOGRAPHER WINFIELD PARKS

BRYAN HODGSON, NATIONAL GEOGRAPHIC STAFF (ABOVE); NATIONAL GEOGRAPHIC PHOTOGRAPHER GEORGE F. MOBLEY (OPPOSITE, ABOVE); AND JOSEPH S. RYCHETNIK

"Longest paper route in the world" engages Bob Reeve, president of Reeve Aleutian Airways (opposite). The veteran of 37 bush-flying years bundles hometown papers—collected for him by airline pilot friends throughout the Lower 48—for shipment free to men in the lonely Aleutians. As a young flyer (in portrait) he devised glacier landings, and hauled supplies ranging from dogfood to dynamite to far-off mining outposts. Helicopters become taxis on remote Amchitka Island, where modern-day frontiersman Ben Morris (above) ferries workmen and hardware to U. S. Atomic Energy Commission test sites. A Coast Guard pilot (below) flies a photo-patrol mission to observe alien fishing fleets. Reliable weather reports and ra-dio beacons aid today's aerial challengers of Alaska's vastness.

and thrashed its way into Lake Grosvenor. Ray had planned to set me ashore to fend for myself and return to his other guests for the night, but the temptation to test the fishing proved too great. He hauled out his tackle, and we headed for the near bank of the stream. We soon found ourselves enveloped by a soothing, primeval silence marred only by the occasional splash of a trout, the muttering of a raft of ducks, and the far-off, ghostly complaint of an owl. In six casts Ray had two rainbows ranging from 3 to 5 pounds and a lake trout weighing 6 pounds; he seemed almost disappointed to have caught his limit so quickly.

I slept that chill autumn night as though I had been drugged, for the rustlings of woodland life speak to man's deep need for the wilderness. Next morning, tracks in the sand showed that a young moose pursued by two wolves had passed within five feet of my window without disturbing me.

For breakfast I gathered two quarts of boletus mushrooms to go with a fillet of broiled rainbow trout and fried trout roe. As I ate, I wondered pityingly how my colleagues back in the Nation's Capital had breakfasted that morning—probably on a quick cup of coffee and a few bites of day-old Danish pastry before dashing off into the frustrating tangle of rush-hour traffic.

Damp rot captures a bunker that the enemy never reached. Moldering World War II helmet and mess gear bespeak soldiers' haste to leave the lonely Amchitka outpost where only storms came to break a foggy monotony.

I found myself caught in a traffic jam at Cold Bay—gateway to the Aleutians—350 miles down the Alaska Peninsula. The sole bottleneck bulked smaller than a Volkswagen, but blocked the road more effectively than a Sherman tank. Spending the night at Cold Bay while waiting for a plane to take me out the Aleutian chain, I stepped out of the lodging house after nightfall to go to dinner. After a few feet, my eyes adjusted somewhat to the dark and I came to a jolting halt, for in my path loomed a black blob that swayed ominously.

Mustering all my powers of concentration, I willed my eyes to pierce the darkness, and I made out a bear facing me threateningly from 20 feet away. Interpreting my paralysis as determination not to back down, the bear gave up first in what he apparently thought of as a contest of wills and shuffled off to the garbage dump. The dining-hall crowd dismissed the encounter as nightly routine.

Next day at the airport I witnessed an extraordinary manifestation of the casualness of Alaska's bush airways. The plane dispatcher announced that a mixed cargo-passenger flight had just been pulled together for a round trip to the Pribilof Islands, 325 miles to the northwest in the Bering Sea. He invited any passengers waiting for planes to other destinations to make the Pribilof trip just for the ride. So I boarded with half a dozen Aleuts returning from a two-year stint in the fish and crab canneries of the islands on the southeastern side of the Aleutian chain.

The fewer than 600 Aleuts living in the bleak Pribilofs represent nearly one-third of this almost vanished people who once numbered perhaps 16,000 or more. They live by killing and skinning fur seals during the annual hunt supervised by the Bureau of Commercial Fisheries, or by working in canneries farther south.

The Pribilofs share with the Aleutians a reputation for suffering the world's worst weather. Terrible winds blow over treeless moors, and fogs hide the sun for weeks on end. We descended through storm clouds and made a landing approach through turbulence that threw me about in my seat with bruising jolts. A freezing gale blew snow horizontally across the cheerless field, but the instant the ship had come to a shuddering halt and a door opened on the leeward side, the Aleut passengers leaped to the ground with little cries of joy and threw themselves into the arms of waiting relatives. I shivered in the partial shelter of a tin-sided shanty, the only structure at the airfield, till the pilot signaled me to board. I promptly obeyed, and we took off for the return flight to Cold Bay.

In the spring of 1943, a quarter century before my visit, Cold Bay had been a staging area for the assault on Japanese-held Attu Island, at the far end of the Aleutians. Seldom have American troops gone into battle with less knowledge of the conditions they would face. The only available map of the island, a Coast and Geodetic Survey chart, showed terrain features for only a thousand yards inland from the shore. Little more was known about the harbors, and aerial photographs of the fog-shrouded bastion filled in few gaps. Estimates of the size of the Japanese force, first tabbed at 500, eventually rose to a possible 1,600 to 1,800; but even the top figure remained substantially short of an actual enemy strength of 2,400.

The weather proved inhospitable from the start for the attack force of 11,000 — drawn from the 7th Infantry Division — delaying the departure from Cold Bay by 24 hours. On May 4 the convoy moved out, although a chilling rain still pelted the stormy sea. As the ships drew closer to Attu the weather grew increasingly worse. Dense fog, rain, and high seas forced postponement of the attack by a day, and then another.

Finally, with no prospect of improved conditions, commanders ordered the landings to begin on the third day, May 11, despite the fact that they would have scant air support.

So began the fight to retake Attu, a battle that raged for 18 raw, muddy days. The end came on the night of May 29, when the remaining Japanese force — between 700 and 1,000 men — charged into the American lines in a final banzai, or suicide, attack. The attack failed, and the next day the Japanese announced the fall of the island, having lost their entire force.

Our troops counted 2,350 enemy dead; only 29 were taken prisoner. But the battle had been costly for the United States, too. Of a force that had grown to more than 15,000 by the time the campaign ended, 549 had been killed, and 1,148 wounded. Another 2,100, many of them victims of foul weather and inadequate clothing, had been put out of action by illness or nonbattle injuries. The nearly forgotten battle of Attu ranks second only to the assault of Iwo Jima as the most costly of the war for this Nation: For every hundred of the enemy, 71 U.S. soldiers had been killed or wounded.

Attu saw the only ground fighting of World War II in North America. Two and a

Wildflowers bloom on a common grave of Japanese killed on Attu in North America's only ground battle of World War II.

Overleaf: Moor-rimmed Atka village huddles beside the quiet waters of Nazan Bay. Under Russian rule, the island hamlet served as an outpost for fur traders. The few Aleuts who remain eke out a meager subsistence by catching salmon and hunting seal and caribou.

half months later, on August 15, U. S. troops also landed on Kiska, but they met no resistance. The Japanese had slipped away by ship three weeks earlier.

Today, except for a small Coast Guard loran station on an otherwise unpopulated Attu, airmen on Shemya — 35 miles to the east — man the farthest west outpost on American soil. With special permission from the Air Force, I flew there.

Radar antennas too big to hide stand on the hilltops. The small, windswept island lies only 500 miles from the coastline of the Kamchatka Peninsula, where the Soviet Union maintains an all-weather naval base at Petropavlovsk. Although the Air Force station does track satellites, its basic mission remains classified.

Everywhere on the tiny island, once a bomber base, the debris of war makes the dreary landscape seem even more bleak and inhospitable. Half-buried in the moor for better protection from the bitter winds, Quonset huts — quickly abandoned with the coming of peace — rust away from the rains of a quarter century. At the foot of a cliff lie toppled casemates still housing 3-inch cannon.

In many areas of Alaska the empty oil drum befouls the landscape, but on those islands where the military has passed, oil drums threaten to crowd man himself out of large areas.

At Shemya I met Robert D. Jones, Jr., then manager of the Aleutian Islands National Wildlife Refuge, a 4,250-square-mile tract taking in all but 7 of the 207 islands of the chain. Shemya's 1,150 airmen, cooped up for a year on the four-mile-long, treeless island, have made pets of hundreds of arctic blue foxes. The creatures have become so tame that when NATIONAL GEOGRAPHIC photographer George Mobley lay on the ground to capture the sun setting behind a radar antenna, he was overrun by a swarm of foxes playing tag across his back, pulling at his pants legs, and licking his face and the lenses of his cameras. Even George, who has the ferocious disposition of a fuzzy puppy, batted and slapped furiously at the foxes.

Bob watched with a sour expression.

"These foxes came to most of the Aleutians only in the first decades of the last century, planted by fur farmers and allowed to forage for themselves," he said. "They wiped out the native bird populations before turning to the sea and the sand hoppers on the beach for food. And, of course, these Shemya foxes thrive on a supplementary diet from the Air Force garbage dump. Only tiny Buldir Island 80 miles from here still harbors a small flock of the almost-extinct Aleutian race of Canada goose, destroyed everywhere else by these intruders.

Fog half hides a giant drilling platform on Amchitka Island as the Atomic Energy Commission prepares for underground tests of nuclear warheads for anti-ballistic missiles. Drillers use a mammoth burred bit (above) to bore 10-foot-wide holes thousands of feet into bedrock.

Furry treasure, bewhiskered sea otters (opposite) float in kelp beds off Amchitka. Dark thick pelts once prized by mandarins caused conflicting claims of empire. Hunted to near-extinction by 1900, small herds now thrive under federal care. Otters feed on sea urchins, and sometimes rock to sleep tethered by a twist of kelp. But nuclear tests have not disturbed their refuge.

Plump horned puffin clings to a windswept Aleutian cliff (above). At breeding time the male puffin puts on a clownlike face and prepares a nesting burrow with its stubby beak. Below, thick-billed murres perch on a rocky cliff, guarding their eggs; the conical shape of the eggs offers a built-in protection, helping to keep them from rolling off the ledge.

"I don't dare touch the foxes because the airmen in their desperate loneliness have made pets of them. But just let one case of rabies break out and bam! They'll go the same way as the 2,500 blues we killed on Agattu in 1964 for just that reason.

"Then we'll bring back the Aleutian goose and all the rest of the wildlife that has disappeared down the maw of these misplaced foreigners."

On Amchitka, in the Rat Island group to the east, I witnessed the happy results of a conservation program run by unsentimental professionals like Bob.

Waters teeming with sea otters first lured the Russians to the Aleutians in the mid-18th century, but by 1910 a fleet of 16 schooners averaged less than two pelts per ship in a season. The sea otter appeared doomed to join the passenger pigeon and the dodo in extinction. The very next year the trapping nations signed a treaty protecting the sea otter throughout its range on both sides of the Pacific.

For decades professional wildlife managers coaxed the sea otter population back to health. With Baine H. Cater, biologist for the Fish and Wildlife Service, I took

TED LODER

off in pilot Ben Morris's Sikorsky S-55 helicopter for a census of the Amchitka otters.

On a two-hour tour around the 4-by-40-mile island, between patches of fog we counted 2,302 otters floating on their backs in the kelp beds just offshore, idly watching us circle each pod for a careful tally. Baine said that the sea otter has recovered in the Pacific Basin from remnant numbers to perhaps 30,000 or more, with about 3,000 in the largest colony, around Amchitka.

With the cooperation of the Atomic Energy Commission, which is preparing a series of subterranean nuclear tests on the island, the state has transplanted more than 300 otters to southeastern Alaska waters and to the Pribilofs, both areas where the animals once thrived.

During my first visit to Amchitka, the approaching date for underground testing of missile warheads was worrying Bob Jones. "Don't celebrate the sea otter's happy fate until you consider what is going on around the drilling sites," he said. "Personally, I've just about written off Amchitka."

Not far away, drillers for the Atomic Energy Commission, working at the request of the Department of Defense, were pushing down four immense holes. At one hole — planned for a depth of 6,050 feet — I watched a crew rig a bit that weighed 300,000 pounds, counting the "doughnut" sinkers designed to give the drill extra bite. The bit measured a gigantic 10 feet across; oil-well drills, by comparison, run a skinny 6 to 8 inches in diameter.

Between my visits the AEC had fired one underground shot of more than one megaton — 50 times the Hiroshima blast. Members of Federal and state wildlife agencies were clearly delighted to report to me that they found the effect on wildlife had been negligible.

So Amchitka's sea otters continue to provide a reservoir for restocking the Pacific coasts where they have disappeared.

Wilderness signature: a river's course scrawled across treeless moors. Brushed by restless Aleutian clouds, shining Shishaldin Volcano rises from Unimak Island. With the arrival of summer, bright heads of Alaska cotton, or Eriophorum *(above), light the green bogs.*

THOMAS J. ABERCROMBIE, NATIONAL GEOGRAPHIC STAFF

F ROM THE CAB of the diesel-driven AuRoRa—the capital letters stand for Alaska Railroad—I helped the train crew keep a lookout for moose. Enough snow had fallen to attract the giant browsers to the railroad right-of-way as a convenient route to fresh pasturage. "We're likely to encounter moose anywhere between the outskirts of Anchorage and Curry, 130 miles to the north," engineer Dennis O'Neil explained. "When I spot one I slow down and try to scare him off the track with loud blasts of the train horn. Generally he gives in."

But not always, I learned. Now and then a recalcitrant bull tries to contest the AuRoRa Streamliner's right to the track in a superb but usually terminal display of courage. Section hands along the way inherit the job of dressing the carcass for delivery to a charitable institution, in accordance with railroad policy.

I was bound for Fairbanks, inland terminus of the federally owned Alaska Railroad, 356 miles north of Anchorage. The state's second city, Fairbanks serves as the main trading center and unofficial capital of the interior, that vast expanse of rugged country—much of it unpopulated—that lies between the Alaska and the Brooks Ranges.

Every few miles during the early part of the 12-hour run, homesteader couples stood beside the tracks and waved as we approached. Following a milepost-by-milepost schedule of flag stops passed to him by conductor Harland Holtan, Dennis either slowed the train to let the homesteaders throw mail aboard or stopped to unload groceries and supplies the isolated residents had ordered from Anchorage by mail or radio.

At one point the train stopped to pick up a mother and her four children en route to the nearest section house, 17 miles away, for weekly baths all around. They would spend the night and ride back the next day on the southbound AuRoRa. Farther along, a hunter held up a crudely lettered sign reading, "Pick me up tomorrow at Milepost 212," and the conductor made a note in his agenda. I remembered from my visit to Seward that all mileposts along the route read in error. The Good Friday earthquake and accompanying seismic sea waves chopped a hunk off the Seward end of the line, and Mile .0 is now actually Mile 1.4.

Along the right of way, footprints left by teeming wildlife coming and going on their incessant errands cluttered the snow cover. Here and there a stain of blood and tatters of fur showed where a woodland tragedy had been played out between fox and hare. Cabins in the scrubby woods marked lonely homesteads. From some, trails of smoke rose slowly skyward; many others long ago had been abandoned, left to the moose and lynx.

A highway parallels the tracks but motorists still cannot drive directly from Anchorage to Fairbanks because of a vexatious 5.5-mile gap north of Mount McKinley National Park requiring several major bridges.

After listening to railroaders' shop talk and gossip about the homesteaders, I moved back through the train to see if the same cozy ambience prevailed among the passengers. I counted only eight fare-paying customers, most of whom stayed in the club car. An Eskimo from the Seward Peninsula and another from the Kuskokwim delta amiably argued the merits of their different dialects. They hooted with good-natured derision at each other's accent and called on me to judge the relative melodiousness of their different speechways—a difficult task, for all Eskimo dialects employ throat-cracking consonants, croaking gutturals, and half-strangled sounds most unmusical to the unhabituated ear.

As Mount McKinley came into view all my new acquaintances in the car, with that

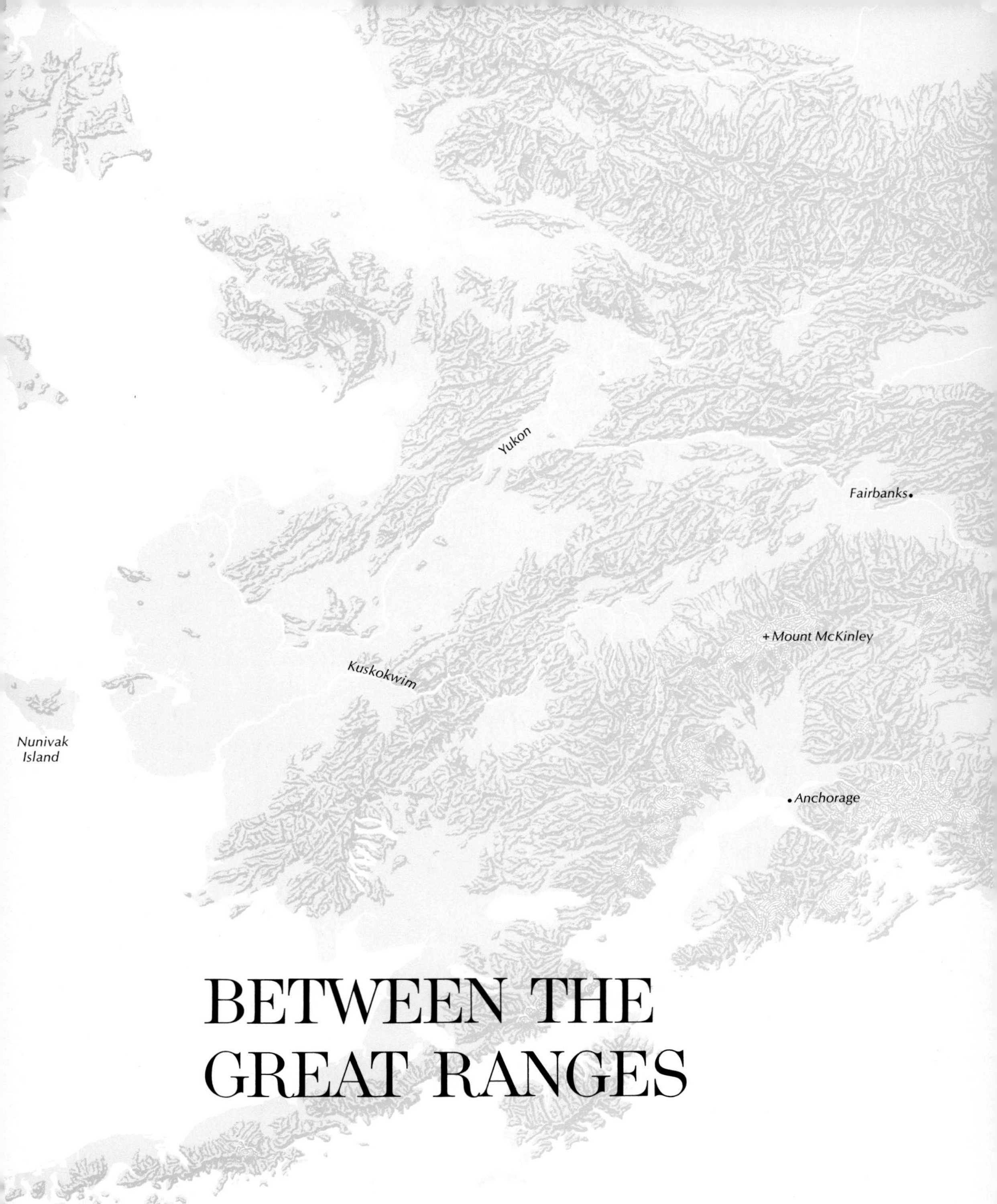

Nunivak
Island

Yukon

Fairbanks.

+ Mount McKinley

Kuskokwim

. Anchorage

BETWEEN THE
GREAT RANGES

5

Alaskan compulsion to claim all superlatives for their state, assured me that it ranks second only to Mount Everest for height. Two years earlier I had traveled for the National Geographic Society through the Gilgit Valley of disputed Kashmir, surrounded by 60 peaks higher than McKinley but so puny in the stupendous Karakoram Range that they didn't even rate names.

To the Alaskan travelers, however, I said only that they were mistaken, that McKinley thrusts some four-fifths of its 20,320 feet from the surrounding terrain, a more dramatic rise from foot to summit than most mountains in the world, including Everest. They gloated visibly at their mountain's promotion to championship rank.

We had been climbing steadily since leaving Talkeetna—more than 900 feet in 60 winding miles. At Milepost 279, climaxing a six-mile-long picture-window view of McKinley, we passed within 46 miles of its towering twin peaks. Still we climbed. At Milepost 310, the AuRoRa crested the continental divide at 2,363 feet, and we rolled by Summit Lake—a body of water that performs the astounding feat of draining simultaneously into the Bering Sea to the west and the Pacific Ocean to the south, on either side of the divide.

Thirteen miles beyond, we crossed Windy Creek, southern boundary of the 3,030-square-mile Mount McKinley National Park, which offers a haven for 37 species of animals and 132 species of birds. Of the latter, the wandering tattler wings northward from as far away as New Zealand to spend its summers in the park. The ptarmigan, on the other hand, remains in the north the year around, switching from a brown-and-gray to a white plumage with the coming of snow; three species, the willow—Alaska's state bird—the rock, and the white-tailed ptarmigan can be found within the park boundaries.

Hunters hail an Alaska Railroad passenger train en route from Anchorage to Fairbanks. The federally owned line operates daily during the summer and twice a week in winter.

More than 33,000 people visit the park annually, lured by the majestic mountain grandeur, unspoiled vistas, and an abundance of wildlife that also includes grizzlies, wolverines, timber wolves, great herds of caribou, and flocks of Dall sheep.

We headed down the northern slope of the Alaska Range toward the great interior basin, the region drained by the mighty 1,979-mile-long Yukon River, third longest in North America after the Mississippi-Missouri and Mackenzie systems. At Nenana—Milepost 411.7—we rumbled across the Tanana River. Here, on July 15, 1923, less than a month before his death, President Warren G. Harding drove the golden spike that signified the completion of the Alaska Railroad.

Alaskans today are much more likely to associate Nenana with the "Big Breakup" that marks the end of winter in the interior. Each year officials rig up a tripod on the frozen Tanana and connect it to a clock on shore. As the ice cracks and shudders and begins to move downstream—usually in early May—the wire linking the tripod to the clock snaps, stopping the clock at the precise moment of the breakup. The

Nenana Ice Classic, a lottery begun in 1917 by a handful of residents to relieve the boredom of a long winter, now draws thousands of participants annually. The winning one-dollar ticket that happens to name the exact day, hour, and minute of the breakup has been worth as much as $125,000.

The rolling, wooded interior gradually merges to the west into a lake-dotted coastal plain of muskeg and tundra. Except for rainfall—in areas away from the sea coast the precipitation scarcely exceeds that of desert Arizona—the region suffers the worst extremes of Alaska's climate. For example, in the Dunbar area, 20 miles beyond Nenana as the railroad goes, winter temperatures may dip to −70° F., and the brief summer may send the mercury zooming toward the 100° mark.

From Dunbar, we rolled northeastward along the north bank of Goldstream Creek and I soon found myself in Fairbanks. I stepped out of the station into the sharp chill of an interior autumn night. Overhead, luminous arcs and bands crisscrossed the darkened sky like sweeping beams from giant searchlights.

"Look," said my taxi driver, "the northern lights are welcoming anyone fortunate enough to be visiting Fairbanks for the first time."

Along the outskirts of the city I had seen modestly handsome housing developments similar to those in any Lower 48 city of 15,000. In town, however, log houses of sturdy pioneer construction still stand among more modern buildings, indicating how close the city lives to its frontier past. Some Fairbanks residents still chink their drafty log houses by boiling up great clouds of steam that leak through the cracks and freeze in a winter-long seal.

Along the downtown streets, parking meters leaned at tipsy angles, an aftermath of the disastrous Chena River flood of 1967. I learned later that Fairbanks winters offer at least one distinct bonus: Parking meters do not work well below −20° F. and conk out hopelessly at −35°.

To me, one of the best bonuses granted to the city by its northern site lies in the growing complex of arctic studies institutes at the University of Alaska campus and the many resident

AuRoRa engineer Dennis O'Neil, a veteran of 35 years with the railroad, knows everyone who lives along the flag-stop route. Bull moose occasionally contest the right of way.

and visiting scholars who give the isolated subarctic city a highly intellectual flavor.

The university, situated on a hilltop rising from the Chena River floodplain four and a half miles west of Fairbanks, offers its 2,700 students a curriculum with the usual fare of advanced studies plus such arctic specialties as Athapaskan language courses, creative writing in Eskimo, management of wildlife on the tundra, and engineering in regions of permafrost. The school even acts as landlord to a band of musk oxen.

While trying to communicate the next day over the exasperating Fairbanks telephone system—many people blame the flood for maddening cross-connections and wholesale blackouts—I idly watched a table lamp rock on its base. Concentrating on interpreting a succession of unearthly dial tones, I remained only half-aware that table lamps do not dance unaided.

But as my chair slid two feet across the floor, I suddenly realized—an earthquake! I already had been toying with the idea of following the (Continued on page 142)

Against a psychedelic backdrop (opposite), an Eskimo student from the University of Alaska performs at a Fairbanks youth center. An eerie skyglow above marks the release of barium vapor from a rocket-borne cannister 600 miles above the earth, part of a university experiment aimed at tracing magnetic fields. Domes house cameras and instruments to record changes in the cloud made visible by ultraviolet light from the sun.

Aurora borealis dances above the tree-hemmed campus of the University of Alaska, a major center for studying the solar-spawned phenomenon. Streaking the nighttime polar skies, the northern lights display a shimmering variety of patterns, such as pulsating single arcs (opposite) and sweeping multiple bands (above and below). Eskimo children whistle to bring the luminescent fingers closer, then quickly flee indoors before the heavenly specters snatch them into space to use them as footballs.

'The Great One'
MOUNT McKINLEY

"Like looking out of the very windows of heaven," Bradford Washburn—one of the first climbers to conquer Mount McKinley—said of the 100,000-square-mile view from atop the highest peak in North America. Monarch of a rugged realm, the 20,320-foot mountain reigns majestically over a 3,030-square-mile national park. Below the 3,000-foot timberline, forests of spruce descend toward the tundra, where in summer tiny forget-me-nots bloom beside meandering streams. Haven for 37 species of mammals and 132 kinds of birds, the park draws 33,000 visitors annually to gaze at the peak that Indians centuries ago named Denali—the Great One.

Overleaf: Silver-frosted peaks and ridges of Mount McKinley stretch upward to a summit hidden behind wispy clouds. Glacier-fed streams weave across the lush lowland at the mountain's base.

NATIONAL GEOGRAPHIC PHOTOGRAPHER GEORGE F. MOBLEY

BYRON S. CRADER

GEORGE HERBEN

Big-eared moose calf, a park pet.

Ground squirrel, a proficient panhandler.

Angry jaeger (opposite), a summer migrant from Pacific islands, swoops past photographer Suzy Loder with a raucous clamor to warn her away from its nest in Mount McKinley National Park.

Talkeetna sourdough self-reliance rails at an outrage — incorporation. Treks up Mount McKinley begin in this tough little town, a whistle-stop on the Alaska Railroad that typifies small Alaskan settlements: unpaved streets, clapboard buildings, and a fierce pioneer pride among the citizenry. Alice Powell, owner of the Talkeetna Motel, presides over a candle-lit dessert table (upper left). Phil Brandl and Eddie Barge sluice for gold at Cash Creek (left). Bush pilot Don Sheldon (right) flies climbing parties to Mount McKinley, 75 miles away.

DO YOU WANT THE
SELF-APPOINTED
"PROTECTORS" TO
MANAGE TOWN AFFAIRS
TALKEETNA IS ONE OF THE FE
PLACES LEFT WHERE WE CA
LIVE AS REAL INDIVIDUALS!
LET'S KEEP IT THAT WAY
VOTE AGAINST
INCORPORATION!

BRYAN HODGSON, NATIONAL GEOGRAPHIC STAFF (ABOVE); JOSEPH S. RYCHETNIK (OPPOSITE ABOVE); AND NATIONAL GEOGRAPHIC PHOTOGRAPHER GEORGE F. MOBLEY

Mountain-climbing by helicopter, sightseers peer into a primeval high-altitude world of ice, snow, and stone. The setting sun peeks past Mount McKinley, out of view at left, and burnishes two jagged summits. Dead ahead, Ruth Glacier flows past craggy ridges of the Alaska Range, a 600-mile-long arc of mountains—averaging 8,000 feet in height— that slopes to the Gulf of Alaska. Nimble as a mountain goat, a turbine helicopter with an altitude capability of 20,000 feet (right) clings to a precarious foothold in full view of McKinley. In 30 minutes the chopper conquers sheer alpine walls that would take earth-bound explorers weeks to scale. Aircraft aid mountain climbers in Alaska by vaulting deep crevasses and landing on glaciers to place teams closer to their goal. The rest of the way, the climb becomes an ageless struggle of man against cold, storm, fatigue, and diminishing oxygen.

BRYAN HODGSON, NATIONAL GEOGRAPHIC STAFF (ABOVE), AND LINDA BARTLETT

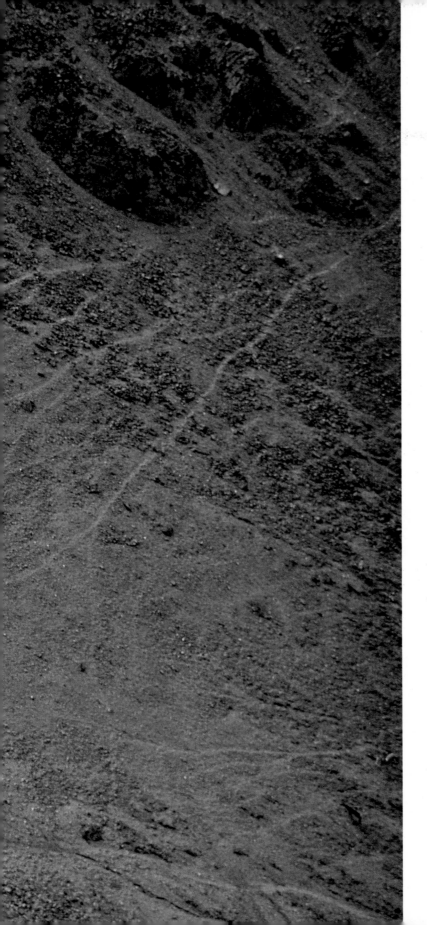

Milling caribou crowd onto a mountainside snow patch to escape troublesome warble flies, diminutive pests that deposit eggs on the legs and flanks of the stately animals. Restless and spirited, caribou travel hundreds of miles in seasonal migrations. Each spring a herd of about 5,000 moves across McKinley National Park to calving areas on the lower slopes of the refuge. In July, they course back down the mountains to feed on lichens and mosses near Wonder Lake, at the northwest edge of the park.

GEORGE HERBEN

Parisian and Mexican practice of dealing with similar telephone systems by calling in person. The jelly-like shimmy of the floor under my feet convinced me; I headed out under open sky toward the University of Alaska campus. Keith Mather, director of the famed Geophysical Institute, told me the earthquake hit 6.75 on the Richter Scale, a score of vastly greater magnitude than the 10 to 20 microshocks—people do not sense many of them—that shake Fairbanks every day. When I confessed, somewhat sheepishly, that the quake had been more than enough to frighten me, Keith replied, "Don't feel bad. When the books started tumbling off my shelves during the Fairbanks earthquake of 1967, I dived under the desk. I felt foolish under there, but I didn't come out till I was certain the shaking had stopped."

But no matter how unsettling such tremors may become, they attract a number of geophysical scientists to this far-northern center of advanced education.

"Alaska has had just about as many surface earthquakes as any region on earth, and any seismologist will tell you where you've had one major quake you'll have another," Keith said. "It may take 200 years of waiting, but you can bet there will be another big one. Seismologists, like other students, want to go where the action is.

Cousins of the Rocky Mountain bighorn, Dall rams laze on a lofty rock ledge in McKinley Park. Each dark ridge in the animals' graceful horns records a year's growth.

"For the same reason, many of the world's best students of auroral activity and the earth's magnetic field are drawn here. Where else do you go? Some polar studies go forward at Kiruna, Sweden; in scattered observatories in Norway and Siberia; and at a site in Saskatoon, Saskatchewan; but at the University of Alaska the serious polar scientist finds a concentration of students in many disciplines and a constant cross-fertilization among the sciences. The whole state offers a magnificent geophysical laboratory with high magnetic and high geographical latitude, a spot right under the aurora, thousands of square miles of glaciers, and the beautiful Arctic Ocean— beautiful for a scientist, I mean.

"Where else can you build a house on the ocean for your comfort and storage of your instruments, chop a hole in the front yard, and study marine biology at your leisure?"

Many scientists such as those who fish through the ice for knowledge work at the Institute of Arctic Biology. I talked with the eminent Dr. Laurence Irving, the institute's advisory scientific director and professor of zoophysiology. With his graduate fellows, Dr. Irving was working on the puzzle of how naked seal flippers, caribou noses, beaver tails, wolf pads, and bird legs operate at temperatures far too low for nerve function in warm-blooded animals.

"Arctic land mammals remain warm-blooded animals only in their central core. The cold flesh of naked extremities acts as an insulator to prevent too rapid a radiant loss of heat from the vital centers," he said. "Now we have to learn what keeps the nerves working in those cold extremities."

Dr. Irving introduced me to John Baust, a graduate student in charge of some of those neurological experiments. Standing 6 feet 4 inches tall, John bent his 220 muscular pounds to the meticulous task of attaching wire electrodes too fine to be seen to nerve endings in the brains of stump beetles. He then takes a series of electroencephalograms of the insects' brains.

"We can follow a bug's thoughts summer and winter," Dr. Irving said. "Nerve endings should not operate at −12° C. [+10.4° F.], but arctic insects don't know that, so they go right ahead. The implications have importance for human beings, especially for deep space probes."

My mind flashed to the space travelers sleeping in deep freeze in the movie *2001: A Space Odyssey*. While visiting Alaska's several arctic-studies centers, I repeatedly ran into matter-of-fact preparations for suspended animation of human beings during interplanetary voyages.

"Glycerol levels in the blood of arctic insects climb rapidly as winter approaches," the scientist explained. "We have used glycerol in modern times as an antifreeze and a preservative for tissues at subfreezing temperatures, but beetles discovered glycerol eons ago. They even overdo the protective bit, for they can survive in liquid nitrogen at −150° C. [−238° F.], a temperature that even Fort Yukon scarcely approaches with its −71° F. record."

Dr. Irving only reluctantly concedes that Eskimos and Athapaskan Indians of the interior may have some physiological advantage in braving the cold. "Mostly they have better techniques for living with the cold," he said. "But they may undergo a gradual hardening process with the onset of winter; however, the only evidence we have hardly ranks as scientific.

"When I directed the Naval Arctic Research Station at Point Barrow, we kept a tame gull around the lab. Somebody left the door untended, and the bird wandered out into a 30-below-zero storm. His brother gulls who were caged outdoors screamed

Stealthy lynx prowls in search of a winter meal. Its wide-track paws equip the lazy hunter for greater speed over snow; long, muscular legs help to provide pouncing power.

with pleasure in the gale, but the pet collapsed with pitiful cries in three minutes. The skin peeled from his frozen feet, and he could not walk for weeks."

At Eielson Air Force Base, 26 miles southeast of Fairbanks, Air Force instructors teach air crewmen of all the services how to survive if they are forced down in the arctic winter. During my visit to the base, the night temperature had already dropped to −16° F., easily cold enough to make me shiver, but the school's seven instructors grumbled that the weather barely sufficed for good training.

"We never cut off training, no matter how low the temperature goes, and we've never had one case of frostbite," said SM/Sgt. William C. Barbour, then chief of the school. "What we teach here ensures that a downed airman will be able to survive with minimum equipment under the worst conditions."

Each airman in the arctic travels with a 45-pound survival kit containing food, signal devices, extra clothing, a sleeping bag, knife, saw and hatchet, fire makers,

BRYAN HODGSON, NATIONAL GEOGRAPHIC STAFF

Doomed Athapaskan Indian village of Minto, 44 miles west of Fairbanks, lies beside its now-quiet nemesis — the Tanana River. Frequent floods inundate log homes in the background and destroy vegetable gardens. Descendants of nomadic hunters who once roamed the interior, 4,700 Athapaskans now forsake tribal life to live in cities, or, like the people of Minto, combine summer jobs in construction and forestry with winter hunting and trapping. But living off the land does not

144

STEVE AND DOLORES McCUTCHEON (ABOVE), AND LINDA BARTLETT

provide today's necessities. Thus, Minto's official population — 380 — contrasted with the actual number of residents — 200 — tells a story of an old day dying, and new ways shaping the lives of Athapaskans. Chief Peter John (left), 84, a lifelong resident of Minto, hopes a planned relocation of the community away from the river will halt the exodus. The bright eyes of six-year-old Angela Charlie (right) may well see a future far different from life in the village of her birth.

145

Tamed as a pup, wolf Gemini accompanies Joan Koponen on her rounds of the family homestead near Fairbanks. A special permit allows the Koponens to keep Gemini (above right), a playful pet with a taste for soap. Moose Josephine (above left) visits the Edward J. Dolney farm during the winter to beg handouts; daughter Karen offers a hamburger bun.

and a life raft. Most of them carry extra gear of their own choosing in flight-suit pockets—candy bars, gimmicky knives with tools attached, fishing line and lures, and protected kitchen matches. Instructors pound away at two cardinal rules: Set up a comfortable camp immediately; never attempt to walk out.

"We used to run a hunting and fishing camp," Sergeant Barbour said, "but now we teach the men to make a warm shelter first and live on their emergency food stores till a search plane finds them. They help the search by laying cut branches in geometric patterns to catch the eye of air patrols and by heaping brush for a signal fire."

Four crews of about nine men each were at work building camps in the woods. Using parachute panels, spruce boughs, fallen trees, and layers of snow, students built A-frames, lean-tos, and pup tents—one-man shelters of every shape that availability of material and ingenuity suggested. S/Sgt. John A. Rehr conducted me on an inspection tour of the shelters his students would sleep in that sub-zero night.

The sergeant was pleased. "Ah, a delightful shelter," he said. "Ideal, ideal. This fellow should spend a comfortable night.

"And look at this clever student. To cut off the biting wind, he has filled his parachute bag with snow and fitted a lanyard to it so he can pull it after him and cork the entrance to his little home."

Following the inspection tour, we sampled the survival rations—dried cornflake bars, dehydrated potato bars, and desiccated soups. Sergeant Rehr said he liked the cornflake bar best. As gracefully as I could, I declined his invitation to spend the night, and hurried back to town, where I assured my own survival with a crab cocktail and a London broil.

During dinner I pored over a mass of clippings I had gleaned from issues of the Fairbanks *Daily News-Miner*—columns of news tidbits from correspondents in native villages all over the northern part of Alaska. I read and re-read the items, delighted by their honesty and freshness.

From Selawik, in the far northwest, an Eskimo wrote the glad news that the caribou had finally arrived on their annual migration, and hunters had raced toward the east to bring down a winter's supply of meat. An unfailing Eskimo hospitality prompted these charming lines: "...one female Caribou real visit right to village, but she went away without any hurts, because she is visitor to our village."

And extending the same spirit to his readers, reporter Ray P. Skin tried to attract tourists by a tantalizing account of Selawik night life: "In this village we have juke box in two places also some times Bingo games...."

From Chalkyitsik, near the Yukon border, J. H. Herbert launched a jeremiad on the morals of his generation: "...there's no one to go out to trap this fall. All they do is get a little wood for each day and I don't think no one wants to trap."

He further lamented that "Drinking is going again tonight," and named the brewer of homemade beer and the cronies who helped him consume it.

Henry Shavings, reporting from 20 miles across Etolin Strait, off Alaska's western coast, lured me to Nunivak Island with his accounts of the reindeer and musk oxen herds that ramble that frozen wildlife refuge.

My plane to Nunivak carried me down the Kuskokwim River valley that slopes southwestward to the Bering Sea. The pilot's chart showed dozens of villages along the riverbank, leaving the impression of a populated territory, but a glance out the window at the bleak countryside showed more lakes than people.

A⊤ MEKORYUK, the only remaining village on the 1.4-million-acre island, half the population of 300—alerted by the airplane's circling—came to the beach to welcome whoever was arriving. Children scrambled to see who would carry my luggage to the guesthouse and guide me next door to the dining room where I met Delbert Neuhart, supervisor of the reindeer roundup and slaughter for the Bureau of Indian Affairs; Dr. William Searles, veterinarian and meat inspector for the U. S. Department of Agriculture; Kazuo Uoi, from Tokyo; and Henry I. Wang, a Korean.

The presence of a supervisor and veterinarian made possible not only interstate shipment of reindeer meat, but also export to other nations, such as Canada and Japan. Gradually, during a dinner conversation carried on in fractured English, the purpose of Mr. Uoi's and Mr. Wang's visits also became clear.

From Mr. Uoi I learned that Japanese do not like to eat meat that has become discolored; he hoped to find a way to treat reindeer carcasses so that they would arrive in Japan looking as if they had been newly slaughtered. Also, he planned to extract juices from the soft antlers and muscles of handsome, freshly killed bulls. Two Japanese research firms would then turn these extracts into peptides for test consumption by aging men seeking to restore their waning vigor.

Mr. Wang told me that he buys and processes reindeer antlers for sale throughout the Orient as an aphrodisiac. Next morning I found him crouching beside a black cast-iron wash pot heated by smoldering bits of driftwood. As he stewed a mess of reindeer horns, he showed me how they would be sliced with other organic materials into a prescription for the Asian pharmaceutical market.

At the slaughterhouse corral 1,000 reindeer of the island's herd of 10,000 milled about wild-eyed, grunting with terror, clashing antlers in senseless fights born of frustration. Sorting chutes led run-of-the-mill animals into the slaughterhouse line, but superior specimens passed through an escape gate toward freedom to build the herd. On their way back to the tundra, they had to run a gantlet of Eskimos who daubed them with paint for identification on later roundups, castrated most of the bull calves, and dehorned the grown bulls—with no bears or wolves on the island the reindeer need no defenses. Mr. Wang bought the antlers for $2.50 a pound.

Some 750 musk oxen — sometimes called the cattle of the arctic — also roam across the Nunivak National Wildlife Refuge. In my Alaskan travels I soon learned that the herd, nurtured from a stock of 33 yearlings and calves imported from Greenland in 1930, had become the focal point of a giant-size controversy. Increasing numbers of Alaskans — many avowed conservationists among them — had come to favor limited hunting of rogue bulls to curb overgrazing of the range. To other conservation-minded people, however, even the harvest of selected bulls conjured visions of past travesties — greedy hunters, finding the animals easy prey, had shot Alaska's native musk oxen into extinction by the mid-19th century.

During 1968 the state legislature approved a bill authorizing limited hunting, but then Governor Walter J. Hickel vetoed it. A year later, as Secretary of the Interior, Mr. Hickel spoke out strongly against a similar measure that was gaining headway in the legislature.

"It would be a disservice to the cause of preservation and development of our natural resources to allow hunting of these gentle creatures, which have so much potential for domestic development," the Secretary said. He advocated instead the continuation of a program of domestication and the use of the Nunivak herd as a reservoir for restocking other areas of Alaska where the animals once had ranged.

The legislature approved the bill, nevertheless, acting at the request of the state Department of Fish and Game. The measure set a cost of $500 for licenses granted to resident hunters and $1,000 for nonresidents.

Experiments have since been conducted in restocking musk oxen in remote areas they once roamed to determine if herds can, indeed, be made to thrive again. In 1969

Overleaf: Alarmed musk oxen on Nunivak Island form a defensive semicircle. Hunters shot the gentle, shaggy beasts into extinction in Alaska before the United States took possession of the territory. The present herd has grown from stock imported from Greenland in 1930.
RICHARD T. WALLEN

Eskimo foreman Jack U. Williams (opposite) wrestles a reindeer marked for tagging, dehorning, and return to the herd at the annual Nunivak Island roundup. Hero-worshipers (below) long for similar prowess. Islanders butcher about 1,000 reindeer a year and export the meat.

the state, with federal aid and the help of the Air National Guard, airlifted 52 young cows and bulls in plywood crates more than 1,000 miles from the Nunivak refuge to Barter Island for release in the Camden Bay area on the Arctic Coast. The animals were tagged and coded with colorful plastic streamers to help with identification.

Because of the musk ox's fancied resemblance to a bison, the buffalo nickel is known to many Eskimos as a *muskoka.* And as domestic animals those musk oxen may bring a few extra muskoka to Eskimo purses, for they bear a soft undercoat called *qiviut* that could bring as much as $50 a pound for use in weaving luxury garments. Each ox can produce about $250 worth a year, so a man could make a tidy bank deposit by tending even a small herd through a winter.

With the windup of the season's reindeer slaughter, I joined my new-found friends at a farewell supper. Gorging on such Eskimo delicacies as stuffed reindeer heart and boiled tongue, made from jealously guarded recipes, I thought I detected an elusive quality in the cuisine. But just what that quality was evaded me till the pretty Eskimo cook dropped a fork and ripped out a sturdy French oath.

I had been eating Eskimo cooking with a French touch—the latter imported by Marian Scarzella, Eskimo wife of the French former manager of Charles V Restaurant at 53rd Street and Fifth Avenue in New York City, one of my favorite luxury luncheon retreats. Mrs. Scarzella had brought her two sons to the lonely island in the Bering Sea so they would know their mother's culture produced something besides chocolate-coated ice-cream bars. Indeed, Mrs. Scarzella served us her Nunivak version of *agutuk,* so-called Eskimo ice cream, made with chilled vegetable shortening, sugar, and salmonberries, and soused with seal oil—a distinctly ungallic dish. My first encounter with the fatty foods of the Eskimo proved fascinating, but Mrs. Scarzella said I had not truly been tested yet.

"When you get into the real Arctic," she said, "those Eskimos up there will give you something to think about with the food they eat."

Officer of the Alaska National Guard Eskimo Scouts (below left) checks wind and terrain during airborne maneuvers. Over the target, he precedes his men from the plane (opposite). Billowing red smoke marks a drop zone. More than 1,000 Eskimos serve in two Scout battalions, units that trace their ancestry to the Territorial Guard of World War II days.

ALONG THE ARCTIC COAST the summer passes swiftly, and the winds from Siberia bring blowing snow and ocean ice early in the autumn. But to the Eskimo the winter has its charm. In an issue of the *Nome Nugget* I read a report from the newspaper's correspondent at Gambell, on the western tip of St. Lawrence Island, 45 miles from the Siberian coast. Eskimo-speaking Mrs. Joe Slwooko wrote of the changing season in limpid English worthy of a Hemingway at his best:

"... we are all having the time of fall, when the ground is frozen hard, the air is sweet and cold, and the sky seems to be gray with snow showers.... Now the lake is all ice.... The ground is also covered with snow, all white, but at the sea, there is no ice yet. The waves are bringing us little more sea foods, sometimes even the herrings came ashore, when the winds have been strong enough to cause big waves.... We are busy getting ready for cold winter."

At Nome, along the southern coast of Seward Peninsula, my plane descended through a dense curtain of clouds and emerged into a lead-colored northern winter world—a livid sea heaved sluggishly under a livid sky, and on land the snow lay somber gray in a livid light. The little streams that in summer still lure diehard gold prospectors lay frozen over and deserted. Along the glide path, abandoned mining dredges made great splotches of rust and decay against the trackless snow.

6 ADVENTURE

U.S.S.R.

Kotzebue.

Little
Diomede
Big
Diomede

BERING SEA

Nome•

Alaskan gold mining has fallen on evil days, even in this northern outpost born of one of the world's great gold rushes at the end of the last century. The value of all the gold mined in Alaska in 1969 totaled only $881,000, a figure hardly indicative of a prosperous industry. That year Alaska mined one sixty-ninth of the United States' total production.

But the mysterious virus of gold still infects the susceptible. Shortly after my arrival at the North Star Hotel, my local cicerone furtively offered to take me to a dealer in freshly mined gold. At another hotel we slipped upstairs and into a second-story room where I met a miner, his son, and a Levantine type who disappeared quietly soon after my arrival. In keeping with the stealthy atmosphere, the miner asked that he remain anonymous so that his name would not alert thieves who might rob him during his travels.

He opened an attaché case fitted with racks of mayonnaise jars containing nuggets of assorted sizes, from almost dusty fineness to lumpy blobs as big as walnut meats. A dull green natural patina of manganese covered the biggest chunks. The coating comes off easily in a sulfuric-acid bath, but the miner said many jewelers prefer to buff only the highest surfaces and leave the dimples green.

The miner peddles the gold in person, slipping with attaché case from hotel to

IN THE ARCTIC

•Barrow

BROOKS   RANGE

CANADA

hotel through Nome, Seattle, Las Vegas, Los Angeles, and San Francisco, selling to jewelers and rockhounds. To foil robbers, he comes and goes to his market cities unannounced except to a few old customers, and somebody stays in the room with the attaché case at all times.

The contents of the case represented five months of work by the miner, his son, two brothers, and a nephew along 12 miles of leased river 100 miles inland, near Kougarok. Once 3,000 prospectors worked the area, but now only this small band remained, mining gold with seven bulldozers and a pumping plant.

"How much do you figure you've got in the case?" I asked.

"A good $35,000 worth," the miner replied.

I did a bit of rapid calculation on the price of round-trip tickets for the five from their homes in Oregon, the cost of living five months in an area where even beans run 40 percent higher than at their grocery stores back home, the cost of seven bulldozers and a pumping plant and fuel transported a hundred miles into the bush, and the expense involved in peddling the gold in cities thousands of miles apart. I soon understood why gold mining is dying in Alaska.

BOB AND IRA SPRING

Brightly bundled dogsledders pass a winter-idled gold dredge in Nome. High mining costs and a static price—$35 an ounce in the U.S.—make it unprofitable to work most Alaskan deposits.

But I also witnessed the hold that finding raw gold has on some men. The miner's eyes gleamed almost lasciviously as he looked at his precious nuggets. I didn't bother him with my breakdown of his probable profits for five months of fighting mosquitoes on the tundra and seven months of peddling his wares over a fair hunk of North America; he wouldn't have wanted to hear it.

With the decline in mining, Nome's population fell from a high of 20,000 at the turn of the century to 2,300 by 1960. It has climbed back since then to about 2,500, most of the newcomers being Eskimos. Over the years, the entire village on King Island has moved to Nome and built a community on the outskirts of town, where the men spend quiet winter days carving ivory. During my visit women joined the men to dance for a group of tourists. As part of the act, older women exhibited hunting weapons and kayaks and pantomimed their men's hunting for the walrus on the ice floes of the Bering Sea during the spring and fall. As the middle-aged dancers re-counted stories of great hunting feats with stiff, stylized gestures, a group of King Island youngsters drifted into the hall. They stood and watched for a few moments and then drifted out again, looking for more excitement.

Bob Davis, superintendent of the Nome District of the Bureau of Indian Affairs, looks after 9,000 Eskimo charges in an Oklahoma-size territory of northwestern Alaska. He foresees a shrinking domain.

"The educated youngsters don't want to live in the villages," he said. "Already they have formed Eskimo colonies in Chicago and Los Angeles. And when birth control reaches the couples still living in the remote villages, many of these historic little places will shrivel and disappear over a few generations. Even the middle-aged are moving to regional centers like Nome, Bethel, Barrow, and Kotzebue to be near the bureau's schools and hospitals."

At Kotzebue, 175 miles northeast of Nome at the tip of the Baldwin Peninsula, I found additional evidence of growth. The town is enjoying a boomlet in tourism. Visitors from the Outside come to ride dogsleds, fish through the ice, watch Eskimos dance, and to embark on polar bear hunts. In the 28 years before my 1968 visit, the town had grown from 372 to about 1,850, of which 1,500 were Eskimos.

Despite a growing sophistication brought on by tourism, however, Kotzebue still carries many of the marks of the Arctic frontier. On the way in from the airport, I saw a bearded hunter unloading from a truck a still-bloody grizzly hide with head attached. Jumping out of the car, I helped the man, Art Fields, spread the pelt for measurement. A crowd quickly formed to exclaim over the pelt's overwhelming dimensions, and even Art—the slayer of uncounted numbers of bears in his 30 years of hunting—seemed impressed. The skull measured 16⅝ inches long by 10½ inches wide, and the hide measured 7 feet 11 inches in length and 8 feet 7 inches in girth.

Art's trophy clearly ranked among the largest grizzly bears ever taken.

"I've been after that scoundrel for five years," Art said. "He broke into seven houses this winter near Noatak, north of here. He tore the whole side off one building at my gold-mining summer camp—apparently he tried to go through a window rather than an open door. So when snow fell, and I could track the brute, I took off after him. Two weeks ago I hit him in the head with a .30-06, but it just gave him a little headache."

Art showed with the tip of his rifle where the high-powered bullet had glanced off the bear's skull, leaving a pink-and-white furrow already half-healed.

"But yesterday I caught up with him good, and he obliged me by charging. I put three .30-06 bullets into his body before he quit coming."

NATIONAL GEOGRAPHIC PHOTOGRAPHER GEORGE F. MOBLEY

Nuggets remain exempt from price pegging. This palmful would bring about $500 in the jewelry trade.

Art put up the hide for safekeeping from the dogs that make Kotzebue nights hideous with howling and joined me at the "farthest north restaurant in North America"—a typical Alaskan claim that blandly ignored the existence of two others in Barrow, 335 miles nearer the Pole.

The menu gave me a pleasant surprise, listing 42 items from a Golden Whale special salad and a 2-inch-thick New York cut steak to a standard hamburger, which I loathe. Slowly I worked my way through the menu, attempting to order. Of the first 40 items, all were "temporarily" out of stock. In desperation, I asked for a cheeseburger, hoping to derive some gustatory pleasure from the soggy textural interplay of slabs of cheese and ground meat. But the cheese supply also had been temporarily exhausted, so I ordered a hamburger—the last item on the menu—and envied the Eskimos dining that night on seal liver and bear paw.

Art, who has not been farther south than Anchorage in half a century, makes his living flying sportsmen out over the ice to hunt polar bears, cousins of the grizzly.

Taking off with a hunter, Art scours the ice pack of the Arctic Ocean and the Chukchi Sea off the Siberian coast, alert for bear tracks. *(Continued on page 164)*

Nome, Alaska. May 30th 1906.

Memorial Day, 1906: Residents parade through Nome, then in its gold-rush heyday. Carrie McLain (above), who marched in the procession (arrow), has watched Nome change from boomtown to quiet trading center. Dawn finds a sweeper (below) at work on Front Street's wooden walks.

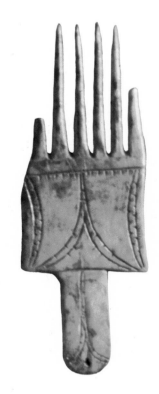

Strength and simplicity characterize Eskimo ivory carvings, an art born in the
sculpting of tools and charms. Punctures
and lines representing facial tattoos scar
an idol (opposite) from the 2,400-year-old
Okvik culture of St. Lawrence Island in the
Bering Sea. The Okvik Madonna (above,
left) clutches a child to her breast. Of all
the Okvik carvings found, she alone smiles.
Incisions endow the child's doll beside her
with magical properties. Woman's comb
resembles those used for preparing grass
for basket-weaving. Carving from Point
Hope (right), done on a whale vertebra,
typifies recent tourist-trade art work.

N.G.S. PHOTOGRAPHER GEORGE F. MOBLEY (UPPER LEFT, LOWER RIGHT,
AND OPPOSITE), AND THOMAS J. ABERCROMBIE, N.G.S. STAFF

Tomcod and Arctic smelt pile up beside a fisherwoman (opposite), and workmen collect blocks of ice to be melted for water, as residents of Kotzebue draw sustenance from their wintry surroundings. In summer, Eskimos from as far as 300 miles away rendezvous at the small coastal village—on the tip of the Baldwin Peninsula—to trade, sing, and dance.

From experience, he can tell by the size of the pad marks if the specimen will make a worthwhile trophy.

Modern techniques call for use of the buddy system, with two hunters and two guides in a pair of planes so that all four can crowd into one plane should the other be forced down. Also, when one guide spots a large bear and lands to begin the stalk on foot, the other plane stays aloft to check for shifting ice and to keep the hunters below informed of the bear's whereabouts. The spotters communicate with the ground party by flying low over the hunters and yelling out the window of the plane.

Good sportsmanship forbids the use of radio communications on such hunts; hence the buzzing and yelling arrangement, even though it may take several passes to deliver a message and make certain it is understood.

But even without two-way radios, such flying forays have evoked criticism from both conservationist and sportsmen's organizations. The Boone and Crockett Club, clearing house for statistical data on North American big game, has removed the polar bear from its list of trophy species. Its Big Game Committee strongly questioned whether aerial pursuit of the animals constituted "fair chase," and said too little was known about the world polar bear population—estimates range from fewer than 7,000 to more than 10,000—to determine an acceptable harvest.

Art gets $2,500 for a ten-day hunt. The hunter also pays transportation to Kotzebue, hotel expenses, and a $150 game tag. The taxidermist gets from $300 to $500 for mounting an open-mouth rug and from $1,000 to $1,400 for an average life-size mount. But such expensive tabs apparently do little to deter the affluent trophy seeker.

Before polar bear hunting became an increasingly popular "sport" in the mid-fifties, the number killed annually over an 18-year period averaged a modest 117—and most of these were taken by Eskimos for food. I checked the tally for 1968 as soon as it became available; the numbers taken during the year totaled 351,

JOHN J. BURNS (ABOVE) AND LEE MILLER

*Spooked by an airplane, a polar bear and her cubs lumber across pack ice near Shishmaref,
on the Chukchi Sea. Polar bears rarely come ashore, spending most of their lives on sea ice.
Increasing numbers of trophy hunters search for the bears by plane, landing to stalk them
on foot while another plane stays airborne and the pilot reports on the animal's whereabouts. Game clubs—concerned by lack of data on the polar bear population—condemn such
aerial pursuit as "unfair chase." Eskimos may hunt the animals for food without restriction,
but take few. At left, frost rimes the back of an old bull walrus. Hvalross, a Norse word mean-
ing "whale horse," gives the mammal his name. Tusks gouge clams and mussels from the sea
floor. His pin-cushion muzzle holds about 400 stiff sensory bristles, also used to shovel food
into his mouth and to strain rocks and shells. Hide two inches thick covers six inches of blubber.*

three times the average of the "pre-sport" era. And I found that even this startling figure fell substantially short of the 399 killed two years earlier.

Eskimos still may hunt polar bears for food without restriction in Alaska, but fewer and fewer do; of the record total of 1966, they killed only 52. I learned that taking a polar bear no longer commands the prestige it once did in the native society, now that white hunters are able to bag trophies with comparative ease. Also, Eskimos complain that aerial hunting parties, ranging far out over the ice pack of the Arctic Ocean and the Bering Sea, are driving the bear from many of its traditional haunts. Before the state Department of Fish and Game set limits on a guide's annual bag, Art killed as many as 31 bears in a single year. Now he can participate in only six hunts, and this drastically limits his income. "But I see more bears than ever before — 49 in one day last season," he told me.

For the present, Alaska game managers tend to agree with Art that polar bear numbers are not dropping. At least they see no falling off in the average size of pelts and skulls, usually the first sign of a dwindling population. Nevertheless, the trend toward more and more kills worries many conservationists.

While at Kotzebue I received a telegram from Bob Davis in Nome confirming arrangements for NATIONAL GEOGRAPHIC photographer George Mobley and me to go to Little Diomede, a 2¼-by-1½-mile jumble of rocks set squarely in the middle of the 54-mile-wide Bering Strait just 2½ miles from Russian-owned Big Diomede, across the Date Line. This was a trip neither George nor I wanted to miss, for the people of Little Diomede — who for centuries have lived by their *umiaks,* or skin boats, wresting a living from the cold sea — have the reputation of being the Vikings of the Eskimo world.

I reached George by telephone in Fairbanks, and we agreed to meet at Shishmaref, off the northern coast of the Seward Peninsula, where the U.S.M.S. *North Star,* supply ship of the Bureau of Indian Affairs, was scheduled to call briefly on October 13 before making its only trip of the year to Little Diomede.

Our plans were simple enough: We would travel to the island aboard the *North Star,* go ashore to interview and photograph the famed sea rovers while the year's

Scientists weigh a drugged polar bear slung in a net from a helicopter — part of a study on the physiology, ecology, and population spread of Thalarctos maritimus. *Ice beards a bear made tipsy by a harmless tranquilizing agent (below left). Researchers also measure and tag the animals (below right); tags aid in tracing migratory habits of the polar bear.*

LEE MILLER (ABOVE LEFT AND OPPOSITE) AND JIM BROOKS

supply of fuel oil and food staples was being off-loaded, and then return with the ship to its next mainland port of call.

My bush pilot had no trouble lining up the runway at Shishmaref. So close to Santa Claus's home, the tallest tree growing on the tundra, the creeping willow, stands only inches high, so the villagers import their Christmas trees. Flown in by bush plane, the trees represent a tidy investment, and after the holidays villagers make extra use of them by sticking them into the snow to mark the sides of the landing strip.

T HE WHOLE VILLAGE had assembled on the beach for the biggest festival of the year, the arrival of the *North Star*. Children racketed through the crowd, for *North Star* Day is too highly charged with excitement for youngsters to follow school routine. The keen eyes of an Eskimo schoolboy first picked up the tip of the supply ship's superstructure piercing the horizon. Snow squalls periodically blotted out the ship's approach, sending the children into despair, but the young adults bustled about getting boats ready for the lightering of next year's stores.

Among the half-dozen metal-sided boats, one skin-covered umiak stood out because of its graceful design. Its framework presented a marvel of ingenious handicraft. Bits of whalebone, carved walrus ivory, strips of driftwood, and lashings of walrus sinew formed ribs, struts, thwarts, a harpooner's knee-rest in the bow, and a steersman's transom in the stern.

"Shishmaref has owned this umiak since I can remember," one of the men told me, "and I was born in 1918, so it has been around a long time. But Diomeders built it, and with a new walrus-hide covering every three years or so it will last forever." When the villagers shoved off from the beach to begin lightering, the elite crew chose the skin boat over the modern metal-sided craft. The fuel oil came ashore first, then the groceries, including staples of all kinds — canned fresh milk, evaporated milk, butter, canned whole chickens, apple juice, syrup, oranges, canned peaches and cherries, even oatmeal cookies.

And this particular voyage of the *North Star* also carried special cargo for Shishmaref — 32 new pews for the village's Lutheran Church.

As the umiak made its final run to the ship, George and I rode along. Capt. Walter S. Hammond welcomed us aboard, and we sailed for the Bering Strait.

The Siberian and Alaskan coasts converge on the strait like the sides of a funnel. When we made our landfall on Little Diomede, for one of the few times in Captain Hammond's 22 years of sailing arctic waters he had a clear view of the Siberian headland of Mys Dezhneva, the Alaska mainland coast at Arctic Lagoon, the Diomede islands, and even Fairway Rock, beyond the islands, at the meeting of the strait and the Bering Sea.

While we were in the chartroom with Captain Hammond, a squall blew up. George and I climbed into a lighter in the dark to ride to the island on a choppy sea in blinding snow.

We leaped ashore and sprinted up the boulder-strewn slope to keep from being hit by the boat's bow ramp, crashing on the rocks as the sea tossed the lighter about. The heaving vessel gave an agonizing shriek as it backed off, scraping its iron bottom. We watched the driving snow swallow the lighter only 40 feet offshore, and turned to greet a party of Diomeders, who escorted us to the school to meet Mr. and Mrs. Maurice McCullen, then schoolteachers for the Bureau of Indian Affairs.

Mr. McCullen, a tall, bald-pated retired accountant from South Dakota, hustled us in from the storm. "I hope you brought your toothbrush," he said.

For a couple of journalists who had planned a fast look around and a dockhead jump back to the ship, the remark had an ominous sound.

"The skipper of the *North Star* just called me by radio to say the lighter barely made it back through the storm, and he is worried about dragging anchor and going aground on the rocks. He has to leave you here and sail for other ports down south."

"When will he come back for us?" I asked.

"You'd better worry instead *if* he'll come back for you. If the storm ends before the cake ice comes down from the Pole, he'll pick you up and unload our supplies. Otherwise, we'll get an airdrop of emergency rations, and you'll stop with us for a few months till the strait freezes solid and a skiplane can come for you. Even the Diomeders can't take you to the mainland through fast-running cake ice."

So began days of measuring winds and scanning the northern horizon for the first dread signs of ice. And the food supply dwindled daily, for the walrus had not yet come down from the north, and the staples left during the *North Star*'s last visit fast ran out. We ate strange combinations as Mrs. McCullen struggled — with considerable success at first — to dramatize the ragtag remnants of her larder. For days we had Jell-O and canned whipped cream. Then we tried a diet of pancakes with salmon-berry jelly. Coffee drinkers soon suffered another deprivation when the store manager sequestered the last dozen cans of evaporated milk for baby formulas.

Adults were finally reduced to eating dehydrated potatoes. The alternative amounted to ten one-gallon jugs of peanut butter, but I had been forced to live on nothing but peanut butter for 11 days during the Great Depression, so I faced up to dehydrated potatoes with courage, at least for the first few meals.

In desperation a crew put an umiak into the water to make a run for food for the children, but the boat turned back almost immediately, defeated by the high seas. The famed boatmen of Diomede showed no inclination to run any more risk just to get George and me to the mainland. They stayed quietly within their houses built from sod, wood, and rock, hiding from the gale and carving walrus ivory and bone into bracelets, effigy walruses, letter openers, and cribbage boards. The schoolhouse rocked from the windy blasts; waves crashing on the beach drenched the building with torrents of green water.

An Eskimo electrician from Unalakleet, marooned with us on the island, poked about the schoolhouse and found a movie projector and several reels of film. In the newsreel, the late President Eisenhower assured his public that the current recession would soon yield to the vigorous attacks of his Republican administration, and Ted Williams trotted around the bases after hitting his somethingth home run. When the Eskimo projectionist threatened to run for the fourth time the movie *Hong Kong,* starring a youthful Ronald Reagan as a ruthless soldier of fortune, George and I looked up Johnny Iyapana, unofficial headman of the village, and offered him steadily escalating sums to put a skin boat into the water and take us the 24 miles that separated us from the world.

We finally offered enough cash to buy a jet-flight ticket from Washington, D. C., to Barcelona or Copenhagen. But John, a redoubtable character of widespread fame as a courageous seaman, and of at least the normal amount of commercial acquisitiveness, still refused to travel in the raging sea, so we resigned ourselves to waiting out the storm in the hope that the polar ice would be late.

On Little Diomede, the Russian presence weighs heavily. With a powerful telescope at the Eskimo Scout armory up the mountainside, guardsmen watched Russian soldiers at an observation shack across the way, and the Russians in turn stared back

North Star *Day—a momentous annual event at Shishmaref—
means full larders for another year to Eskimos of the settlement.
Operated by the Bureau of Indian Affairs, the ship ranges through
northern latitudes delivering food, fuel, and medical supplies to isolated villages. A grinning elder (opposite) helps off-load material
from the vessel. Above, men wrestle a walrus-skin* umiak *ashore. For
the rest of the year, contact with the outside world comes via mail,
flown in to the little Post Office (below) two or three times a week.*

through their glasses. The two groups exchanged occasional friendly waves. As we scouted the beach one afternoon to see if the storm was washing in any interesting flotsam like fossil walrus ivory or precious bits of driftwood, an Eskimo youngster yelled a warning and pointed to the west. Two Russian helicopters flying formation braved the high winds to hover over the international demarcation line, close enough for us to see the pilots studying us through glasses. They landed out of sight on Big Diomede's interior. At breakfast, the best classical music came from Siberian stations, and even the midmorning Siberian pop music — sounding somewhat like Trini Lopez singing a Muscovite mariachi tune set to balalaikas — beat the interminable football games on the few Alaska stations we could pull in.

At first George and I had scanned the waters uneasily in fear of seeing the first walrus pod transiting the interisland channel, for that would mean the cake ice was pushing southward close behind. But after the fourth day of desiccated potatoes, we

joined the silent watch of the Diomeders in hoping to catch sight of the red-blooded edible sea mammals. A loaded rifle stood beside the door at every house in the village.

During a desultory game of Scrabble in the schoolhouse kitchen, my Eskimo opponents and I were jolted out of our lethargy by a 5-year-old boy who burst into the room crying "Walruth . . . Walruth."

Mrs. McCullen, keeping her vigil from the second-floor window, had first spotted a pod of four walruses coming down the channel, and already men were rushing about the village, propping rifles across barrels and upturned umiaks, waiting for the unsuspecting creatures to come within range. A young walrus with the incurved tusks of a female blew for air only 100 yards off the beach, and the volley sounded like the height of the Battle of the Bulge.

Bullets tore the water all about the walrus's head and at least one hit, for blood spread rapidly and the wounded animal in its agony spun on the surface like a top. A huge old cow, experienced in the ways of Eskimos, heroically braved the rifle fire to swim to the little wounded cow, put a huge flipper on her head, and tried to push her under the surface and out of sight. The rescuer paid with her life for her heroism; her ponderous body sank beneath the waves with a bullet through the head. The little female thrashed her life out as she drifted close to shore.

Eskimos whirled grappling hooks on long lines around their heads and hurled them into the sea till they had snagged the walrus. The men of the village threw themselves on the line and hauled the carcass up on the rocks. I found myself with hands clutched around the rope, teeth bared, groaning with heaving lungs from the strain of pulling the beast ashore.

Knives flashed and the carcass began to disintegrate under their attack. John Iyapana presided over the portioning of shares, passing out the bounty with strange

Framework of an upturned umiak stands out boldly against its translucent covering as author Bern Keating plods through October snow on Little Diomede island; Eskimos whittle boat ribs from driftwood and whalebone. The sturdy craft carry hunters far out to sea in search of seal and walrus. Hanging seal hides (above) will be made into boots and trousers.

Hungry for fresh meat, a Diomede villager (opposite) whirls a grappling hook to snag the season's first walrus, a female killed offshore by rifle fire from the rocky beach. Neighbors (above) haul in the sea mammal for butchering. Village leader John Iyapana (below) supervised distribution of the carcass. Little Diomede and Russian-owned Big Diomede (background, above) flank the Date Line in the middle of the 54-mile-wide Bering Strait. Today on Little Diomede is tomorrow on Big Diomede, a scant 2½ miles away.

stiff ritualistic gestures of blood-drenched hands and arms. He set aside portions for the old women who had no men to hunt for them and for the sick who could not be on the beach for the butchering. Within 20 minutes of the time the walrus's muzzle touched the rocks, the village dogs were licking up the last remnants, and all trace of hunters and hunted had disappeared.

John had allotted Mrs. McCullen the liver as prize for spotting the pod, and George and I wolfed down the fresh meat at dinner that night with an enthusiasm unequaled even by that of the Eskimos. And to our delight, we discovered that walrus liver rates among the world's great culinary treats.

But when we had eaten our fill, the depressing thought of the ice floes following close behind the walrus settled over us once again. Then suddenly the radio crackled to life, and the *North Star* reported a slight abatement of the storm.

"We'll be by tomorrow to try to put supplies ashore," the radioman said.

George and I were standing on the beach with luggage at hand when the *North Star*'s bow peeped around the headland. We lent a hearty hand lifting an umiak off its storage rack and carrying it to the water. Paddling enthusiastically till the outboard motor took hold, we suffered drenching with no complaint as the skin boat labored through the angry sea.

A Jacob's ladder dangled over the *North Star*'s side, but even when the skin boat swept six feet upward on the crest of swells, the lowest rung dangled far above foot reach. With the desperation born of ten days of dried potatoes, I leaped for the ladder at the top of a swell and pulled myself up hand over hand till I could engage my feet and clamber to the ship's deck. George followed scant inches behind.

Once aboard, we threw over a heaving line and pulled up our luggage, and George joined me as I broke into a chorus of the old Negro spiritual, "Free at last, free at last, I thank God I'm free at last."

Led by a sympathetic chief steward, we filed into the galley for a snack of cold cuts to hold our appetites while our steaks were cooking.

Diomede mother brings home her share of the apportioned walrus. Below, a storm that marooned the author and photographer for ten anxious days gathers over the island. Had winter ice arrived before the North Star's *return, their exile might have stretched into months.*

"The earth is the Lord's, and the fulness thereof ... for he hath founded it upon the seas, and established it upon the floods." A priest recites the 24th Psalm at a Russian Orthodox funeral at

Kasiglook, an Eskimo village near Bethel. Grief etches the faces of mourners carrying icons to the cemetery. A patriarchal cross (center) bearing the dead villager's name will mark his grave.

Diomede's inaccessibility and the vagaries of the walrus migration have kept the people there in the grip of a constant fear of famine that once haunted the whole Eskimo world. But elsewhere, even though many Eskimos live in the worst slums in North America, they no longer fear starvation.

During my stay with the whale hunters of Point Barrow, I gourmandized on Eskimo delicacies and discovered many table delights new to me under highly improbable guises. Mrs. Harry Stotts, the half-Eskimo wife of the white weatherman at Barrow, rummaged about in her locker and brought up two kinds of muktuk—all-white pickled skin and blubber of the beluga whale, and raw, frozen skin and blubber of the bowhead. Her three adopted Eskimo children crowded about eagerly to claim their frozen bowhead. Striped a waxy chocolate-and-salmon color, and with a rich nutty flavor, muktuk has the same addictive effect on me as salted peanuts. Long after I felt uneasy from overeating, I still popped frozen slices into my mouth.

I asked Mrs. Stotts if she ever cooked the bowhead muktuk, and she expressed horror, saying only a savage would commit such a barbarism.

I munched on *inaluak,* dried seal intestines, and found them good. Whale brains made me think of gray scrambled eggs. A piece of dried caribou intestines packed into the caribou stomach for winter storage is called *ichawrak.*

Portions of fermented seal flippers seemed to grow in my mouth as I chewed them, so I adopted the Eskimo gourmet's trick of chopping them with my teeth once or twice to release the flavor and gobbling them down.

The dishes multiplied, but most of them were based on the principle of anaerobic fermentation—the same process that produces old-fashioned barrel dill pickles and sauerkraut. A piece of *tukta,* made by folding over a flap of walrus hide and blubber and sewing the edges airtight to permit airless fermentation, has a pleasing acid flavor and leaves a tingling sensation on the tongue like a good champagne.

Later, as we dined at the cafe downtown, Mrs. Stotts could not watch me eat a sirloin cooked rare because of her horror of underdone steak.

Barrow's Eskimos live more comfortable lives than most of their race. Two movie houses each have two showings nightly and the young people dance every night in the orchestra pit of the Polar Bear Theater till two in the morning—with a live rock band three nights a week. The matrons play bingo nightly, and sports fans attend two and three basketball games a week.

And all hands have been freed forever from the backbreaking task of scouring the tundra for willow twigs to burn through the winter to ward off the polar cold. For just inland from town, oilmen have discovered a large gas field and the town has fuel to burn.

On my second visit to Barrow I discovered a new aristocracy, the hard-hat Eskimos who spend alternate weeks working as roustabouts at the Prudhoe Bay oil strike on the Arctic coast, earning wages they never dreamed possible.

Under a September sun, a Nunivak Island mother and her son (opposite) gather what they call salmonberries for Eskimo ice cream— agutuk *—made with seal oil, vegetable oil, and sugar. A swimmer (above) rests on an icelike Styrofoam float, imported as packing material.*

CHINA

U.S.S.R.

JAPAN

7   THE

T HE NORTH SLOPE OIL RUSH had just begun when I first visited Alaska in 1968. In February, Atlantic Richfield Company, drilling on land leased jointly with Humble Oil & Refining Company, brought in its first well, Prudhoe Bay State Number One. Four months later came the confirmation strike. Soon responsible geologists were estimating reserves of up to ten billion barrels — approaching twice the size of the east-Texas field, previously the largest in North America.

Flying in and out of Fairbanks that fall, I saw scores of oil workers going to and from the slope, their rock-hard faces and picturesque arctic clothing evoking memories of other boom times. Speculation about a new prosperity swirled everywhere, and Alaskans thrilled to the message humming in the air: Good times a-comin'!

Led by ARCO, Humble, and BP Alaska Inc., oil firms with interests on the slope banded together to build a 790-mile-long pipeline to carry the new-found crude from Prudhoe Bay to Valdez, on Prince William Sound. Despite its price tag of more than a billion dollars, the line seemed the most practical means of transport, for it could pump two million barrels a day at full capacity.

To haul that much oil overland — given the existence of an all-weather highway or rail line linking the slope with central Alaska — would require a fleet of 60,000 tank trucks or daily runs by 126 freight trains. Even counting the costs of constructing a

ALASKA

CANADA

UNITED STATES

FRONTIER. BEYOND

major port facility and operating giant tankers to ship the crude to West Coast ports of the Lower 48, oilmen estimated that the system would be substantially cheaper than a trans-Canada pipeline.

The petroleum consortium—Alyeska Pipeline Service Company—forged ahead with its plans, buoyed by the support of two of every three Alaskans. It launched terrain studies and started to build way-camps along the proposed route across the Brooks Range via Dietrich Pass, over Isabel Pass in the Alaska Range, and through Thompson Pass in the Chugach Mountains. It ordered huge quantities of specially designed 48-inch steel pipe from Japan and signed up scores of contractors, who in turn began moving in thousands of tons of construction and earth-moving equipment.

Pocketing a record 900 million dollars from its 1969 sales of north slope oil leases, the state looked forward to the time when more than 200 million dollars a year in royalties and severance taxes would begin to pour into its coffers. The Golden Age of the Great Land seemed about to dawn.

In the half-light that came before the dawn, however, fighting frigid Arctic temperatures became but a small part of the problem of getting the crude to market. Like Mount McKinley's twin peaks, two huge barriers suddenly loomed in the path of the pipeline: the smoldering issue of unresolved native land claims and

Eskimo snowmobilers of Barter Island, off Alaska's northeastern coast, head home from a Saturday movie matinee in wintry Arctic gloom. An Air Force early-warning radar site provides jobs for many of the island's natives; farther west along the Beaufort Sea, Eskimo roustabouts earn up to $18,000 a year working on Prudhoe Bay oil-drilling rigs. But many of the state's Aleuts, Indians, and Eskimos still live in poverty. Unemployment in native villages often goes as high as 90 percent in winter, and even in summer months seldom drops below 25 percent.

NATIONAL GEOGRAPHIC PHOTOGRAPHER EMORY KRISTOF

a growing concern for the fate of the Nation's environment. Lawyers representing native villages along the pipeline route went to court and obtained an injunction. And conservationists in Alaska and the Lower 48 whipped up a storm of protest over what they feared would be an irrevocable desecration of "America's Last Frontier."

Critics of the pipeline argued that the project would seriously damage the region's permafrost—a layer of ice and frozen soil and rock from 500 to 1,200 feet deep—which remained when Ice Age glaciers retreated from the northern half of Alaska 7,000 years ago. Summer temperatures allow limited growth of sedges, grasses, and lichens in the top few inches of the permafrost called tundra. This fragile layer of soil and vegetation insulates the permafrost against deep thawing.

Conservationists feared that heavy construction machinery would damage the slow-growing tundra cover, ruining it as insulation and causing the permafrost below to melt and create rivers of mud and vast areas of erosion. Others warned that the hot pipeline, if placed belowground, would also thaw the permafrost, again with disastrous results. Still others predicted that a line break caused by an earthquake or a landslide would threaten the region's ecology, and that caribou on their seasonal migrations would not cross the pipeline.

Canadian voices also joined in the argument against the proposal, cautioning against oil spills off British Columbia from supertankers transporting the crude from Valdez to Puget Sound.

Despite arguments against the pipeline, I still found the state obsessed with the frustrated boom on my later visits. Oil dominated conversation in plane and train, bar, parlor, barbershop, hotel lobby, and college classroom. Eventually the oil companies were able to come up with proposed solutions to most of the vexing problems raised by environmentalists, but it remained for the Department of

Steel pipe lies stockpiled near Valdez, on Prince William Sound. Environmental concerns, together with the thorny issue of native land claims, held up construction of a 790-mile-long pipeline to carry crude from Prudhoe Bay to the ice-free port. At Prudhoe Bay (below) snow coats tugboats used to land seaborne supplies arriving during the brief Arctic summer.

LINDA BARTLETT (ABOVE); NATIONAL GEOGRAPHIC PHOTOGRAPHER GEORGE F. MOBLEY (BELOW); AND MICHAEL S. CLINE

Caribou migrate south along a ridge near Anaktuvuk Pass in the Brooks Range; the John River meanders across the valley. Until 1951, the nomadic Nunamiuts trailed the herds across the tundra. Now settled in their village, they still hunt the animals for meat and hides. At left, Arctic John butchers a 275-pound caribou in front of a sod home. Esther Ahgook (right) nibbles on a dried rib.

the Interior to issue a permit to build across Federal lands, working in conjunction with the Environmental Protection Agency and other Government offices. And only the U. S. Congress could decide the native-lands issue.

Many Alaskans considered the warnings of conservationists to be exaggerated, but I had to concede that on my first visit to the north slope I had seen enough evidence of environmental damage to become deeply concerned. I had watched as creeper-tractor operators, made reckless by excitement and lack of supervision, towed equipment trains across the fragile tundra with little regard for the damage they might be sowing in their wake.

In September 1969 I made a second visit to the north slope, this time via the ice-choked Northwest Passage aboard the S.S. *Manhattan*—the ship was testing the feasibility of bringing Prudhoe Bay oil to eastern markets across the top of North America. Snow had not yet covered the terrain, and during helicopter flights over the area I noted obvious evidence of damage to the naked land. It was easy to see where heavy loads had broken through a thin snow cover and crushed arctic plants, exposing the tundra to possible erosion that could scar the landscape for centuries.

F OURTEEN MONTHS LATER I was again in Alaska. Although pipeline construction had been held up, four rigs continued drilling on the north slope against the day when the 50 or 60 wells already drilled and in reserve could be uncapped and put into production. Full of misgivings over what new environmental damage I would find around the oil rigs, I boarded a de Havilland-125 twin jet bound from Anchorage to Prudhoe Bay.

From the air as we circled Sag River State Number One, the confirmation well and main center of activity for the north slope field, I searched anxiously for signs of the carelessness that had disturbed me on my earlier visits.

Not a track disturbed the virgin snow off the paved trails. In the midwinter gloom of near noon, lights from dozens of trucks and bulldozers crept down a network of 50 miles of road insulated with 5 feet of gravel to protect the permafrost. During my visit the temperature climbed to 14° below zero and the wind dropped, making an almost tropical sequel to a storm the day before when gale winds had driven the chill factor to 82 below.

On a tour of the site I learned that drivers suffer penalties if they venture off the insulated roads. Bulldozers cannot lower blades even an inch into the tundra. Covered by drifting snow that offered some protection from the bone-chilling cold, experimental plots test hardy grasses to learn which most quickly will repair damage admittedly done to tundra flora during pioneering days.

Guides proudly showed me the secondary sewage-treatment plant, a more advanced facility than any other in Alaska—except for those of several contractor camps along the proposed pipeline route. Two of the stations even have tertiary treatment plants turning out effluent purer than the drinking water of some cities.

And unlike hideously littered outposts abandoned by the military in the Aleutians or trash-strewn exploratory oil wells I have visited elsewhere in the Alaskan and Canadian Arctic, the campsite at Prudhoe Bay has the severely policed look of a Marine parade ground.

Brenda Itta, an extraordinarily pretty Eskimo girl from Barrow who had joined Atlantic Richfield as a community affairs representative, came along as we toured other camp facilities. Near a stack of 160 miles of pipeline sections, we stirred up three arctic foxes.

"I'd love to have one for my parka," Brenda cried. "I haven't seen a live one since I left Barrow to go to school."

Tom Brennan of ARCO explained that the foxes had once been far more numerous in the camp area, but most had followed a lemming migration to the west.

"A while back we discovered that the insulation of wiring used by seismic exploration crews makes a right tasty dish for a fox. To cut down on short circuits, we brought in a group of Eskimo trappers."

Within a five-mile drive we saw a dozen foxes. I asked how such a barren land could support so large a population.

"It can't," said Angus Gavin, a 30-year veteran of Arctic studies as a former executive vice president of Ducks Unlimited of Canada and presently an ecologist for the oil company. "The men have discovered that foxes are easily tamed and they feed them out the back door on the sly. So we trap them with one hand and nourish them with the other."

Ecological experts like Angus have had to improvise extraordinary solutions to environmental problems introduced by the oil boom. When porcupines developed a taste for the rubberized fabric of 100,000-gallon pillow tanks used for storing fuel along the pipeline access route, they began puncturing the reservoirs with their chisel teeth and spilling the contents. Naturalists now spray tank farms with synthetic weasel urine to scare off the marauders.

During the time of my first visit to the north slope, the mountain of supplies necessary to develop an oil field had been carried almost entirely by air, usually by giant four-engine Lockheed Hercules cargo planes at staggering cost. But on the latest visit I learned that the air transport boom had collapsed, bringing some pain to over-extended entrepreneurs.

Tom showed me docks on the shallow Beaufort Sea. Here lighters deposit the cargoes of deep-draught barges towed thousands of miles in open water from as far as Houston via the Panama Canal, the Pacific Ocean, and the Bering and Chukchi Seas. Crews must rush through the six weeks of arctic summer to bring a year's supply to the outpost.

In the early days of the boom, trucks had supplemented barge traffic, traveling 500 miles from Fairbanks to the north slope on a winter road atop the frozen tundra, crossing the Yukon River on an ice bridge. But the road appeared to have outlived its usefulness. The oil consortium had begun construction of a three-lane gravel highway along the proposed route of the pipeline northward from the Yukon, but I learned that this too had been held up. With the completion of the pipeline, the highway would be turned over to the state.

As I watched Eskimo roustabouts at work, I saw tangible evidence that at least a few of the 52,000 native people already were sharing in the economic benefits that north slope oil promises for Alaska. Too often this has not been the case. Many Aleuts, Indians, and Eskimos — together they make up 20 percent of the population of the state — still live in appalling poverty.

A commissioner of the U. S. Public Housing Administration said, after traveling through the Yukon-Kushokwim Delta, "In the Lower 48 we are trying to get rid of our privies. In some places in Alaska it would be a great advance just to have privies."

In the other states, occupancy of houses averages about one to a room; in Noorvik on the Kobuk River six persons live in each room. Of almost 10,000 Eskimos in western Alaska, only 45 have college degrees; one-fourth have no schooling at all.

Even though the average age at death stays at half the national level, the native

Rising starkly from the north slope—the broad area between the Brooks Range and the Beaufort Sea—an Atlantic Richfield derrick taps a reservoir estimated to contain as much as ten billion barrels of crude; a noonday sun nudges the horizon, barely illuminating a surveyor's work. A parka-clad Prudhoe Bay laborer (left) wears a scarf to protect his face from winter temperatures that often drop to −40° F. Oilmen believe the field eventually will pump two million barrels of crude a day. At that volume, the State of Alaska would gain some 200 million dollars a year from oil royalties and severance taxes.

population grows at twice the national rate, intensifying the already grievous housing problem. Thanks largely to the combined efforts of the U. S. Public Health Service and the Bureau of Indian Affairs, the death rate from tuberculosis dropped from 222 to 6 per 100,000 between 1950 and 1967.

But in contrast to the national average, twice as many natives die from accidents, suicides, and alcoholism, and three times as many from homicide. Influenza and pneumonia kill natives two and a half times as often as whites, and 11 out of every 100 Eskimo children suffer from otitis media, an infection of the middle ear that can cause serious hearing loss if neglected.

Unemployment in the native villages often reaches 90 percent in the winter, and even in summer rarely falls below 25 percent. One man in a dozen earns his entire living by hunting, and one out of two makes at least half his living in this manner. But those who grapple with the native problem do not consider it hopeless. They cite the example of the Tyonek Indians who, with some assistance in solving legal problems, showed real skill at managing a capitalist enterprise — once they got their hands on some capital.

Settlement of the far-reaching land-claims issue could bring a repetition of the Tyonek story in many other Alaskan villages. Acting in concert, the Aleut, Indian, and Eskimo communities have laid claim to virtually all of Alaska. In 1965 the Interior Department froze transfer of any property rights affected by these claims until Congress could find a way to solve the problem. Either through a cash settlement or through recognition of some form of property rights — most notably a percentage of oil royalties and severance taxes — the natives could acquire quite suddenly a considerable amount of money. And the oil boom would be one step closer to resuming its forward drive.

At the University of Alaska I found virtually every department involved in at least one project related to oil and its impact on the state.

The Department of Anthropology has enjoyed some unforeseen benefits. Dr. John Cook, an archeologist who tries unsuccessfully to hide his youthful appearance behind a beard, showed me through a storeroom littered like a pack rat's nest with artifacts gathered earlier that year along the proposed pipeline route.

"With $250,000 in logistic support and hours of helicopter time donated by Alyeska, we completed five years of exploration in one summer.

"Between Fairbanks and the oilfield, we found 200 prehistoric sites. The route passes close to Healy Lake, where in 1968 I found artifacts with radiocarbon dates going back 11,000 years or so, making them among the oldest yet found in Alaska. Already we've uncovered several fluted projectile points on the pipeline route similar to the earliest points from Healy Lake."

Virtually all archeologists now agree that man came to Alaska from the west

Japanese businessmen admire a display of watches at the Anchorage International Airport Duty Free Shop; the entrance (above) greets visitors in two languages. Infusion of vast amounts of Japanese capital to tap rich resources spurs the state's economy. Said one informed Alaskan: "...our future lies just as much in Asia as it does in North America."

during periods when glaciers had so much water locked up in ice that a lowered ocean left a broad land bridge between the Old and the New World.

"The ditch for the pipeline, remarkably similar to an archeologist's transection trench, cuts across one of the major routes of migration from Asia," Dr. Cook said. "We may turn up some of the most exciting finds in the history of the continent."

Alaska's geographical position, straddling the short great-circle route between Asia and North America, continues to exert its influence on the peoples of the Pacific Basin.

Dr. William Wood, the tall and scholarly president of the University of Alaska, drew pictures for me on the back of an envelope one day at lunch. His pencil described a broad arch, and he closed it at the bottom with a straight line.

"This arch represents the basin of the Pacific Ocean north of the tenth parallel," Dr. Wood explained.

Swiftly he sketched in islands and names of countries. "Here at the western base

LINDA BARTLETT

of the arch lies Taiwan, and reading northward you have China, Japan, Korea, and Russia. Starting at the bottom of the other end you have Central America, and the west coasts of the United States and Canada.

"At the keystone of the arch, on the shortest route between any country or combination of countries east and west of the keystone, sits Alaska. So our future lies just as much in Asia as in North America.

"In the Alaska-Japan relationship you have the classic case of complementary societies. The Japanese manufacture about as well as anybody in the world, but they have few raw materials to work with. Alaska has few factories, but raw materials it has in abundance: timber, fish, and iron ore, as well as nonferrous metals, and plenty of natural gas and oil from Cook Inlet already in production—never mind the stalled boom on the north slope," Dr. Wood continued.

The industrial partnership between Alaska and Japan has grown steadily since World War II. During my first visit to Sitka, I called on Atsushi Momma, then resident vice president of the Alaska Lumber and Pulp Company as well as the Wrangell Lumber Company.

The freighter *Sitka Maru* was loading at the pulp-mill pier; Japanese stone lanterns flanked the reception entrance; Japanese-language magazines littered the coffee tables in the anterooms. Along the walls of the conference room where I met Mr. Momma, magnificently dressed Japanese dolls stood in glass cases.

"Since 1959 Japanese have invested about $70,000,000 in this mill," Mr. Momma said. "And we plan to expand. Every year we ship pulp from more than 150,000,000 board feet of spruce and hemlock logs to rayon spinners in Japan. And we have a sawmill in Wrangell producing more than 80,000,000 board feet of timber for export.

Solemn Eskimo children of Anaktuvuk Pass (opposite) share their one-room home with a snowmobile, used for checking traplines. Standing on the breakwater at Nome, Andy Ozenna (above) adopts the stance and attire of modern youth. Settlement of century-old claims to ancestral lands would help ensure a brighter future for Alaska's native peoples.

"For the first three years of its operation, the Wrangell mill lost $960,000, but we invented a way of cutting logs into legally acceptable six-inch-thick slabs with the round arc of the trunk left attached, a cut that opens a huge market in Japan among the small family sawmills."

Alaskan pulp mill operators must be inventive and shrewd to compete on world markets, for the 475 employees of Mr. Momma's mill have the highest pay scale of any pulp mill in the world. The average worker earns $11,000 yearly, with fringe benefits boosting his income to $13,200. Skilled maintenance men make considerably more. The biggest competitor, a joint British Columbian-Japanese pulp mill, pays about half the Alaskan scale.

Conscious of the growing Japanese presence in their area, Sitkans have installed an airport welcome sign printed in Japanese.

In the two years between my first and second visits to Anchorage, I discovered that seven of Japan's great industrial-mercantile conglomerates have opened offices, and the government of Japan has established a consulate. Maurice Oaksmith, director of the Anchorage field office of the U. S. Department of Commerce, told me Alaska projects 148 million dollars in exports for 1971, with 80 percent going to Japan.

"Timber and fish remain the major export to Japan," he said. "But the oil and gas industry is elbowing in. The plants at Kenai ship liquid natural gas and urea fertilizer. At the oil refinery on Cook Inlet, what's left after extraction of jet and diesel fuel goes to Japan to generate electricity. Because the sulphur content runs low, burning Alaskan residual oil adds little to the terrible smog that plagues Tokyo."

Even the ski slopes at Mount Alyeska have felt the Oriental presence. Parties of Japanese now fly in for a weekend on the snow. For those who can afford it, the six-hour flight from Japan beats fighting traffic from Tokyo to the best Japanese resorts.

In addition to the familiar Japanese, other Asians have begun to appear at breakfast tables in Alaskan hotels. The academic, cultural, recreational, and commercial communities in Alaska all are beginning to feel quickened interest from the western shore of the Pacific Basin.

W ITH OBVIOUS PRIDE, Dr. Wood reported that his campus has become a central point for international conferences on high-latitude problems.

"Participants attacked problems concerning disposal of solid wastes, quality of water, public health studies, and survival of the polar bear. We have been host to 14 nations, including scientists from alpine Switzerland and Austria who have quasi-arctic conditions in their high altitudes. And we were especially pleased to have contributions from Russian scientists, for they represent a formidable corps of experts and technicians with enormous backgrounds in arctic studies."

At the Institute of Arctic Biology, the director, Dr. Peter Morrison, told me he had just returned from a precedent-breaking meeting with 200 Soviet environmental physiologists at Novosibirsk in Siberia.

"The Russians searched out the eight foreigners present for friendly conversation. With me, they began tentative but serious negotiations to exchange information and visits so we can share knowledge of the Arctic."

Dr. Morrison was one of several biologists organizing an expedition into the ice-covered Bering Sea aboard the U. S. Coast Guard cutter *Glacier*.

"The trip represents just the beginning of what we hope will be a continuing study of the ecological interface between water and ice at the edge of the ice pack. Walruses and seals breed there. Both American and Russian hunters are harvesting these resources, perhaps to the detriment of at least the ribbon-seal population.

"However, we are at a disadvantage with regard to establishment of international management programs. The opportunity for American scientists to work in this region has been extremely limited, whereas the Russians have benefited from the presence of a commercial sealing fleet. The background of knowledge available to us at present leaves much to be desired."

A less contentious interchange with Asians resulted during 1970 in ten tourist trips through Siberia and Russia, originating in Anchorage and jointly managed by Alaska Airlines and Intourist, the official Soviet travel agency. The 12 tours planned for 1971 were scheduled to stop at Khabarovsk, Irkutsk, Tashkent, Samarkand, Moscow, and Leningrad, among other points. Some of the tours include a return flight over the pole so that passengers can boast of a round-the-world trip. In fact, pilots for Alaska Airlines plan to do a 360° bank around the pole itself so their passengers can report having gone twice around the world in a single flight.

S INCE THE WIDELY PUBLICIZED but only partly successful settlement of farmers in the Matanuska Valley during the Great Depression, agriculture in Alaska has fallen into neglect. But on my latest visit to the University of Alaska, I found agricultural scientists vigorously planning farm development based on new-found Alaskan natural resources. By coupling the natural wealth with new technological breakthroughs, scientists hope to make those new riches valuable tools for a yet-to-be-trained class of farmer-scientists.

During my 1970 visit, a C-46 planeload of hogs from Iowa State University arrived at Delta, 100 miles southwest of Fairbanks in the Tanana Valley. A cross between Yorkshire and Duroc boars and Yorkshire, Spotted Poland China, and Hampshire sows, the litters should have hybrid vigor for quick weight gain, according to Dr. Wayne Burton, a marketing expert at the experimental farm. A modern hog house called a bacon bin, containing two decks of living space and insulated with three inches of polyurethane, awaited the first arrivals. Within five years, ten more houses will shelter enough hogs to produce two to two and a half million pounds of high-grade pork annually. Though Delta suffers cruel winters with temperatures as low as 70° F. below zero, body heat of the hogs, with only slight help from butane space heaters, will hold inside temperatures at 65° F. above.

The real innovation of the Delta hog operation lies in the 800 acres of fields already cleared and used for growing barley. Fertilized with urea from Alaskan petro-chemical plants near Cook Inlet, the Delta barley patches produced about 40 bushels to the acre, close to the national average. With only a small protein supplement, probably from fish meal that could also become a profitable byproduct of Alaskan fisheries, the hog farmers plan to be self-sufficient in feed.

A descendant of the Matanuska Valley farming pioneers, Dr. Donald H. Dinkel, head of the University of Alaska Department of Horticulture, outlined for me plans to profit from Alaska's fuel reserves and to outflank the state's agricultural short-comings by moving farm fields indoors and cultivating them with new techniques that smack of "mad scientist" comic books.

Horticultural tests are now underway at two Alaskan locations using General Electric intensive lighting under controlled conditions of environment to produce rapid year-round growth of high quality flowers and vegetables. A series of tests currently being conducted by scientists and commercial plant growers already indicate technical and economic feasibility for many crops, especially where cheap

Alaskan fuel supplies for heat and electricity will become increasingly available in future years.

"Because we won't need the sun any more, we won't have to use the classical glass greenhouses but rather opaque-walled growth chambers where we can control the climate with exquisite precision, pouring on the right nutrients, moisture, gas mixtures, and lighting conditions," Dr. Dinkel said. "We can tailor our environment to the plant rather than vice versa. Using such plant-growth factories, farmers should be able to meet most of the food and flower needs of Alaska during the next decade. Certain high-value crops might eventually be exported to Tokyo or to metropolitan centers in the Lower 48."

I left Alaska in the wake of a vicious storm that reminded me of the Thanksgiving Day blow that had held up my return to the Lower 48 two years before. I had been surprised then, on taking off from Sitka, to see that the vast land had absorbed the storm's fury with hardly a sign of its passing, though already I had heard that 154 million board feet of timber, enough to supply a pulp mill for a year, had been toppled by the winds.

In the clear morning air that followed the storm, the dark forests appeared to march up the mountainside intact. Graceful gulls rode the breeze, searching for silver fingerlings in the sea, and farther out a gam of killer whales flashed across the water's surface.

As my jet zoomed skyward, I turned to catch a last glimpse of the Great Land: big brawny, and intemperate at one moment—quiet and serene at another—and most of all overpoweringly beautiful.

In its forests, along its streams and bays, deep into its mountain ranges far above the timberline, even on the bleakest tundra, I had found an abounding beauty. I had seen the *real* Alaska—the Beautiful Land—still a pristine frontier too big to be destroyed by man's blighting touch. At least till now.

Aglow with pride, Ada Ahgook of Anaktuvuk Pass exhibits a caribou-hide mask her father fashioned for the tourist trade. Below, children of the village return to school after a noon recess. Slowly adjusting to the changing needs of their rapidly developing state, Alaska's 52,000 Aleuts, Indians, and Eskimos seek to preserve the essence of their age-old culture.

Index

Illustrations references, including legends, appear in *italics*.

Additional References

For additional reading, you may wish to refer to the following NATIONAL GEOGRAPHIC articles and to check the Cumulative Index for related material: "Nomad in Alaska's Outback," by Thomas J. Abercrombie, April 1969. "The Curlew's Secret," by Arthur A. Allen, Dec. 1948. "Weather from the White North," by Andrew H. Brown, April 1955. "Along the Yukon Trail," Sept. 1953, and "North Star Cruises Alaska's Wild West," July 1952, both by Amos Burg. "Vanished Mystery Men of Hudson Bay," by Henry B. Collins, Nov. 1956. "Three Months on an Arctic Island," by Joseph O. Fletcher, April 1953. "Alaska's Marine Highway: Ferry Route to the North," by W. E. Garrett, June 1965. "Earthquake!" by William P. E. Graves, July 1964. "Alaska's Warmer Side," by Elsie May Bell Grosvenor, June 1956. "Alaska Proudly Joins the Union," July 1959, and "Lonely Wonders of Katmai," June 1963, both by Ernest Gruening. "Charting Our Sea and Air Lanes," by Stuart E. Jones, Feb. 1957. "North for Oil: Manhattan Makes the Historic Northwest Passage," by Bern Keating, March 1970. "Hearty Folk Defy Arctic Storms," by W. Langdon Kihn, Oct. 1949. "DEW Line, Sentry of the Far North," by Howard La Fay, July 1958. "Far North with 'Captain Mac,'" by Miriam MacMillan, Oct. 1951. "Alaska's Mighty Rivers of Ice," Feb. 1967, and "First American Ascent of Mount St. Elias," Feb. 1948, both by Maynard M. Miller. "Alaska, the Big Land," by W. Robert Moore, June 1956. "Alaska's Russian Frontier: Little Diomede," by Audrey and Frank Morgan, April 1951. "Cliff Dwellers of the Bering Sea," by Juan Muñoz, Jan. 1954. "When Giant Bears Go Fishing," by Cecil E. Rhode, Aug. 1954. "Exploring Aleutian Volcanoes," by G. D. Robinson, Oct. 1948. "Climbing Our Northwest Glaciers," by Bob and Ira Spring, July 1953. "Nomads of the Far North," by Matthew W. Stirling, Oct. 1949. "An Alaskan Family's Night of Terror," by Mrs. Lowell Thomas, Jr., July 1964. "Scientists Ride Ice Islands on Arctic Odysseys," by Lowell Thomas, Jr., Nov. 1965. "Mount McKinley Conquered by New Route," by Bradford Washburn, Aug. 1953. "Photographing Northern Wild Flowers," by Virginia L. Wells, June 1956.

Composition for *Alaska* by National Geographic's Phototypographic Division, John E. McConnell, Manager. This edition printed by Editors Press, Hyattsville, Md., and bound by Maple Press Company, York, Pa. Color separations by Beck Engraving Co., Philadelphia, Pa.; R. R. Donnelley & Sons, Inc., Chicago, Ill.; Graphic Color Plate, Inc., Stamford, Conn.; The Lanman Co., Alexandria, Va.; Lebanon Valley Offset Co., Inc., Cleona, Pa.; and Progressive Color Corp., Rockville, Md.